HAMDULAILA

The Seven Phases of
*Prophet
Muhammad's Life*

OTHER PUBLICATIONS FROM ISPI

The Nature and Structure of The Islamic World
1995

This book presents the Islamic world as complex, heterogeneous, and overwhelmingly positive. Written by Professor Ralph Braibanti, it was well received and introduced into the curriculum at many universities.

Muslims in America: Opportunities and Challenges
1998

This book contains three articles which expound on its title: "Imaging and Stereotyping Islam" by Dr. John Woods; "A Brief History and Demographics of Muslims in the US" by Prof. Asad Husain; "A Pro-active vision for Muslim Americans" by Dr. Javeed Akhter.

American Public Policy and American-Muslim Politics
2000

Articles by Ali Mazrui, Sherman Jackson and Aminah McCloud on the dilemma of political participation and double identity are discussed in an analytical as well as a dialectical manner. One of the points the book makes is that Muslims should actively participate in the political process.

The books may be ordered via regular mail at
P. O. Box 3402 Oak Brook, IL 60522 or e-mail info@ispi-usa.org.

The Seven Phases of
Prophet Muhammad's Life

Javeed Akhter

forward by
John O. Voll

International Strategy and Policy Institute

Copyright © International Strategy and Policy Institute

Printed in the United States of America

First Edition

All rights reserved. No part of this book may be reproduced in any form or by any means, except for the inclusion of brief quotations in articles and reviews, without prior written permission of the publisher.

For information please contact the International Strategy and Policy Institute, P.O. Box 3402, Oak Brook, IL 60522.

E-mail: info@ispi-usa.org. Website: http://www.ispi-usa.org.

ISBN 0-9647204-3-4

LCCN 2001095309

ORIGINAL CALLIGRAPHY BY MOHAMED ZAKARIYA

EDITED BY KHAJA MISBAHUDDIN

DESIGN BY KATE S. HAMMER

I dedicate this book to my parents,

Dr. Ahmed Abdul Razzak and

Mrs. Akhtary Razzak,

who have inspired me always.

Contents

Quote From The Qur'an 5

Abbreviations Used in the Essay 7

Foreword: Dr. John O Voll 9

Editor's Note: Sabreen Akhter 13

Acknowledgments 15

Objectives of the Review 17

Attitudes towards the Prophet Muhammad ﷺ 21

I. The Seeker of Truth 29
   Search for light in a period of darkness (The burden which was breaking your back...)

II. The Recipient of the Mantle of Prophethood
    The Warner and the Exhorter 37
    The Revelation (Wahy) and its immediate aftermath: (Recite! Recite in the name of thy Lord.)

    Excitement and self doubt (First three years)

III. The Stoic Optimist 45
     Open invitation and brazen hostility (Know that I am a Warner...)

     Migration to Abyssinia (Ethiopia) of some Muslims (The first Hijrah)
     Siege in Abu Talib's Tribal Abode (Boycott by the Makkans of Muhammad's ﷺ tribe)
     Reconfirmation of Hope: The Isra'/Mi'raj experience
     Prophet's ﷺ interactions with non-Muslims

IV. The Pluralistic Leader 59
*Unexpected Avenue for Expansion; Hijrah
(Migration to Madinah): (Conditions must be
fair and equitable to all)*

*Contact with the Madinans, the Oaths of
'Aqabah
The Migration (Hijrah)
The Covenant of Madinah (Conditions must be
fair and equitable to all)
Pluralism: The Islamic view
Emphasis of the Community (Ummah) in Islam*

V. The Courageous Yet Reluctant Warrior 69
*A Clear Change in Direction and the Battles for
Survival*

*Change in the direction of prayer (Qiblah)
The Battle of Badr
Humane Treatment of the Prisoners of War
The Battle of Uhud
The Battle of Khandaq (Ahzab)
The Three Jewish Tribes (Banu Qaynuqa', Banu
Nadir, Banu Qurayzah)
Prophet Muhammad as a Military Leader
Qur'an's Emphasis on the "Nuclear Family"*

VI. The Statesman par excellence and the Teacher 89
*The Peace Dividend; Hudaybiyah/Bay'at ar-
Ridwan (Covenant of Contentment)*

*Muhammad ﷺ as a Statesman
Events Leading Up to the Conquest of Makkah*

VII. The Compassionate Ruler and
Spiritual Leader 101
*The Final Phase (Victory with Humility).
("Today I have perfected for you your religion,
and have bestowed upon you My bounty in full
measure...")*

Contents

The Conquest of Makkah
The Near Defeat at Hunayn
Muhammad's ﷺ Disapproval of Superstition
Gender Relationships
The Role of Women in Early Islam
The Tabuk Expedition
Rationale Behind Muhammad's ﷺ Wars
The Pilgrimage (Hajj) of the Companions in the 9th year of the Hijrah
The Fight (Jihad) Against Economic Oppression
The Concept of Jihad (The Noble Struggle)
The 10th year of Migration (Hijrah)/Farewell Pilgrimage (Hajjat al-wada')
The Sermon at the Farewell Pilgrimage
The Final Illness

Does this essay cover any new ground? 123

Appendices 127
Muhammad's ﷺ persona
The Prophet's ﷺ Marriages and his Wives
The Covenant of Madinah
The Treaty of Hudaybiyah
The Message to Heraclius
"And Said the Messenger ﷺ..."
The Sermon at the Farewell Pilgrimage
The Satanic Verses?
Quintessentials of the Islamic Belief System

Primary Sources 165

Secondary Sources 167

Index 169

About the Author 177

*Indeed there is for you
in the Messenger of Allah
an excellent pattern
(Qur'an 33:21)*

Abbreviations used in this essay and the citation of the Qur'anic verses

It is conventional for Muslim writers to use certain terms of respect and endearment when addressing the Prophet Muhammad ﷺ, his companions and other Prophets. This is part of the Muslim etiquette or *Adab*, which may be defined as the genteel culture which evolved over centuries and became universally accepted and practiced over the entire Muslim world. *Adab* informs the social pattern of Muslims, including conversation, ways of interacting with elders and each other, the use of literature, and dress code among other things. The use of these terms of respect does not prevent the scholar from being objective in his analysis or, when necessary, being appropriately critical. However it requires him to do so in a respectful manner, keeping a fair and balanced perspective, and making sure that the critique is honest and constructive. The following is a listing of common abbreviations used in for the various terms of respect.

ﷻ *Subhanahu wa Ta'ala*; Glory to Him the Most High; used with the name of Allah, or God.

ﷺ *Salla Allahu Alayhi wa Sallam*; We pray that 'peace and blessings be upon him'; used with the Prophet Muhammad's name.

؏ *Alayh as-Salam*; Peace be upon him; used for all other Prophets.

The reader should assume that whenever the companions of the Prophet are mentioned it is the intent of the writer to use the phrase "May Allah be pleased with him/her." The phrase is omitted only for better flow of the text.

I have also decided to give the citation of the Qur'anic verses in the body of the text rather than in the footnotes for better rhetorical flow and easier verification.

Foreward

By John O Voll
Georgetown University

The Prophet Muhammad is recognized as having a very significant role in world history. In a widely discussed book identifying the one hundred most important people in history, he is listed in the first place.[1] People view the Prophet from many different perspectives and write about him for many different reasons, and much has been written about him. It is clear that all recognize, whether they write to praise or to condemn him, that he is a major historical personality.

Despite the vast body of works written about the Prophet Muhammad, there are some gaps. In particular, it is difficult to find a short introduction to the life of the Prophet written from the perspective of the believer but which also recognizes the contributions of contemporary scholarship by both Muslim and non-Muslim scholars. Such a work is needed by young adults and people who are unfamiliar with the historical and religious sources, but want to know more about the Prophet and his life. Javeed Akhter has succeeded in writing such a book for the use of Muslims and other interested people in countries like the United States where Muslims need such publications both to help educate their children and also to inform their neighbors.

Akhter's approach is to concentrate on the different periods in the life of the Prophet. The seven phases of Muhammad's life introduce the reader not only to the biography of the Prophet but also to important themes in Islamic life and history. In setting the stage at the beginning of the presentation, Dr. Akhter reminds the reader of the importance of maintaining a balance in the portrayal of Muhammad. While the Muslim reader is aware of the polemic that has been used by some non-Muslims to attack Muhammad and justifiably rejects such falsehoods, Muslims are also reminded that excessive veneration is not appropriate. The Qur'an emphasizes that Muhammad is "aught but a man" (Qur'an 17:93). It is the theme of Muhammad, the exceptional and influential human being, that guides Akhter through his presentation.

It is unnecessary simply to summarize the writing of Dr. Akhter but it might be helpful to highlight some aspects of this biographical presentation. Akhter gives the reader a short but effective portrayal of the time in which Muhammad lived. It was a time of moral confusion and disorganization among the major religious traditions in the Eastern Hemisphere. The most important humans in history have come at such times and the guidance that they provided in times of social and religious turmoil is what gave them their significance in history. It is of interest to note, for example, that all of the first five names mentioned in the list of the one hundred most influential people in history were people who articulated beliefs and concepts for the guidance of humans, rather than being great military conquerors. Four of the five-Muhammad, Jesus Christ, Buddha, and Confucius are commonly identified with the establishment of traditions of morality and faith, while the remaining person is Isaac Newton, whose influence came from presenting a new vision of life and universe.[2]

The power of the major leaders in history comes from their ability to help their fellow humans gain new insights into the nature of life and the universe which can help to resolve the great issues of their times. The truly greatest of these leaders are those who bring a vision that is not simply helpful during their lifetime but is understood by humans over many centuries to be a vision for other ages as well. The great prophets and teachers in history both represent a climax of the prior experiences and the gateway to a new era. These leaders thus fulfill the dual responsibility of providing a culmination, and a critique, of what has gone before and of defining new paths for humanity to follow. For Muslims, the content of this vision and message is revelation from God. The words of the Qur'an are not viewed as being the words of Muhammad. However, Muhammad plays the role of the messenger and he also is the best exemplar of how humans should live within the guidelines of the revelation. It is for this reason that the specifics of Muhammad's life assume importance for all people.

Muslims from the earliest days treasured reports of incidents in the life of the Prophet Muhammad and preserved them. Many of these accounts or hadith were collected and are the basis for later biographies of the Prophet. The hadith collections provide a great mass of details, and many tales were said by medieval Muslim scholars to not be "sound" traditions. However, as one major Western scholar has noted, "through the mass of all-too-human detail there shines out unmistakably a largeness of humanity, sympathy for the weak, a gentleness that seldom turned to anger save when dishonor seemed to be done to God, something even of shyness in personal intercourse, and a glint of humor all of which contrast so strangely with the prevailing temper and spirit of his age and of his followers that it cannot be other than a reflection of the real man".[3] Akhter makes excellent use of the early biographies and stories about the Prophet's life to present an effective account of this "real man" who possessed a true "largeness of humanity".

The seven phases of the life of Muhammad as portrayed by Akhter show a human being who is distinctively human and facing the problems all humans face. The life of the Prophet becomes, as it has been for fourteen centuries, a model for others to follow. At the same time, the full spectrum of experiences in the Prophet's life as described Akhter goes beyond the life experiences of most individuals. Muhammad was both persecuted and victorious. In tribulation, he is seen as brave, kindly, and humble and in victory he is generous and compassionate. As Akhter shows, in the phases of Muhammad's life, he was a warner-exhorter, a warrior, a statesman , and a ruler, and in each of these roles he was successful in fulfilling his mission. It is this multi-dimensional character of his historical role that gave him, for example, the highest ranking in the list of the one hundred most influential people: "he was the only man in history who was supremely successful on both the religious and secular levels".[4]

The biography of the Prophet as presented by Akhter also provides a sound introduction to Islamic teachings. The primary source used is the Qur'an and the result is a good summary of many important aspects of Islam. By focusing on the life of a human being in the framework of guidance from the Qur'an, this biography also helps to highlight what many people have emphasized: Islam is not simply a set of creeds or beliefs, it is a comprehensive way of life.[5] In the seven phases of Muhammad's life, the reader can find how Muslims lived as a small minority in a non-believing society, as participants in a religiously pluralistic society, and as a majority community. The universality of the message of Islam is reflected in the life of the Prophet. Akhter has provided a helpful starting point for understanding both the message and the human through whom the message was revealed.

---

[1] Michael H. Hart. *The 100: A Ranking of the Most Influential Persons in History.* (Revised edition: Secaucus, NJ: Carol Publishing Group, 1992)

[2] The list can be found as the table of contents in Hart. *The 100;* pp vii-x

[3] H.A.R. Gibb. *Mohammedanism: A Historical Survey* 2nd ed. (London: Oxford University Press, 1961) pp. 31-32.

[4] Hart, *The 100*, p. 3.

[5] See for example, the agreement on this point shown by Muslim teachers with very different perspectives; Abul A'la Maududi "What Islam stands for" in *The Challenge of Islam;* ed. Altaf Gauhar (London: Islamic Council of Europe, 1978) especially pp. 5-7 and Fazlur Rahman. *Islam and Modernity.* (Chicago: University of Chicago Press, 1982) especially pp. 14-15.

Editor's Note

Dr. Javeed Akhter's book is unique because he delves deep into the psyche of the Prophet ﷺ and the actual physical manifestations of his thought processes during the different stages of his life. Also, it is invaluable for those who study the Prophet Muhammad's ﷺ life, to shift paradigms and think about the events and decisions in his life in terms of stages of development, instead of merely a string of seemingly non-cohesive, random happenings. Unlike other biographies of the Prophet ﷺ, Akhter, with the deeply personal and human passion characteristic of a true historian, creates not merely a visceral materialization of the Prophet ﷺ, but also a very clear intellectual one.

Clearly, it is near impossible for anyone to fairly describe the reach and significance, the struggles and ultimate success of the Prophet Muhammad's ﷺ life. Dr. Akhter, however, offers a fresh perspective on the Prophet's ﷺ life, and hence, his view is integral to the continued dialectic about the Prophet. One of the most stunning portrayals of the Prophet Muhammad ﷺ I have ever found, and which this book, though through a different style, captures in full, is seen through a verse by the poet Sharaf ad-Din al-Busiri who wrote in praise of the Prophet ﷺ:

> *Like a flower in tenderness, and like the full moon in glory, and like the ocean in generosity, and like time in grand intentions...*

Sabreen Akhter

Acknowledgements

I am indebted to many friends for encouraging me and providing valuable criticism of this work. In particular, I am very grateful to Dr. Asad Husain, former Professor of Political Science at Northeastern Illinois University, Chicago, IL, and Chairman of the American Islamic College, also in Chicago, IL, for persistently motivating me to write this essay. Former Vice Chancellor of both Aligarh Muslim University and Osmania University in India, Syed Hashim Ali, was both enthusiastic about the project and provided important insights. A bright young man, Syed Mohiuddin Ahmed, provided some very useful suggestions.

Professor John Voll was kind enough to initially review the manuscript and later write a foreword for it. His comments provided me the scholarly peer review I was looking for.

My oldest daughter, Nausheen's, good judgment and keen eye were invaluable in giving this manuscript its current shape. I am also grateful to my wife Naheed's support that sustained me in this project.

Finally I would not have completed this project without Allah's mercy and grace.

Javeed Akhter
October, 2001
Chicago

Objectives of this Review

Scholars as well as the ordinary person in the West are starting to show an understanding and appreciation of Islam and its belief system. However their knowledge of Islam's Messenger, Muhammad ﷺ, his personality and the nature of his mission remains woefully inadequate. Muslim scholarship on this subject has largely focused on anecdotal details of his life, and descriptions of his personality. Only sporadic attempts at analyzing and understanding the dynamics of his life have been made. Trying to gain insight into the "why" of his actions, rather than merely detailing the "what" and "how", is essential in extracting true lessons for those who have an interest in his complex and inspiring life. An understanding of Muhammad's ﷺ actions and the context in which they occurred is also essential in truly comprehending the message of the Qur'an, and what Islam is all about.

The objectives of this analytical essay are twofold:
- a. To stratify his life into various "phases" based on the changing nature of his struggle.
- b. To attempt an analysis of the internal dynamics of his mission and extract its relevance to the current human situation.

Muhammad's ﷺ life is uniquely different from those of the founders of the other major world religions in that he experienced all the trials and ease, hope and despair, near defeat and total victory that any human being can possibly experience. Rather than simply expounding theory and laying out principles, he was able to demonstrate through word and deed how one would act in different situations in life. These life experiences can be divided into various "phases," which are quite distinct and different from each other and are therefore clearly demarcated. An understanding of these phases can provide precedent, hope, and solace to those who seek to comprehend and learn from his mission. The fact that among the major religious leaders of the world, Muhammad ﷺ was arguably the only one who lived in the light of history makes this an achievable objective. A review of these well-defined broad phases in his life, rather than particular incidents, is perhaps of better use to us today. In all of the phases, he remained the exemplar of ideals outlined in the Qur'an and an individual who set standards by his practice which all humanity could aspire to achieve. These phases may be briefly summarized as follows.

First phase: *The "the seeker of truth" deeply troubled by the problems facing humanity.* The early part of his life before the initial revelation (*Wahy*) experience. In this phase, he was deeply troubled by the status of society and spent much time pondering over it.

Second phase: "*The recipient of the mantle of prophethood/ the warner and the exhorter".* The revelation and its immediate aftermath were a period of both great excitement and torturous self-doubt.

Third phase: "*The stoic optimist".* During the period of open invitation to Islam, brazen hostility was generated toward it. He exhibited inspiring optimism while faced with the great frustrations of excruciatingly slow progress in the spread of his message. This period ends with the ascension (*Mi'raj*).

Fourth phase: "*The pluralistic leader".* An unexpected avenue for the expansion of Islam opened with his Migration (*Hijrah*) to Madinah. A highlight of this phase was signing the covenant of Madinah which exemplified his inimitable statesmanship and set standards for pluralism.

Fifth phase: "*The courageous yet reluctant warrior".* This phase is marked by a clear change in the direction of his mission, both literally and figuratively, and the battles for survival (Badr, Uhud, Khandaq). The local Jewish communities played a crucial and tragic role in this phase.

Sixth phase: "*The statesman par excellence, and the Teacher".* In this phase, he signed a peace treaty with the Quraysh and reaped its dividend. In this phase he exhibited the foresight and perspective to compromise and accept apparently humiliating conditions for peace. However, this quickly turned into his greatest victory. These few years of peace were marked by the largest increase in conversions to Islam. He proved himself as adept at being an administrator and lawmaker in peace as he was a leader and strategist in war.

Seventh phase: "*The compassionate ruler and spiritual leader*". In this final phase, he consolidated the remaining objectives before his death.

Although I have used numerous sources in compiling this essay, I have used the Qur'an as the primary and major source for the events of Muhammad's ﷺ lifetime. The Qur'an is essential to understanding Muhammad's ﷺ mission (*risalah*), just as the knowledge of his struggle is invaluable to understanding the Qur'an. His contemporaries often characterized him as the living embodiment of the Qur'an. The Qur'an and the Sunnah, in fact, are as essential to each other as the body is to the soul.

Additionally in this review, I have kept in mind the Prophet's ﷺ own admonition about any attempts at deifying him; "Allah condemned the Jews and the Christians, because they built places of worship upon the gravesites of their prophets."[1] Muhammad ﷺ was very conscious of keeping a clear distinction between his words and the divine words that he received through the revelatory experience. He made certain that no one confused one with the other.

Finally, in discussing the 'seven phases', I am not attempting to demonstrate any type of parallelisms with the number seven, as is done in some Islamic mystical literature. (Seven heavens; seven orifices in the human head; seven visible planets; seven intervals of a musical octave; seven days in each quarter of a lunar cycle). I could have used the words "many" or "various" however, I settled on "seven", as it appeared to be the most direct way of characterizing the results of my analysis.

---

[1] Muhammad B. Isma'il al-Bukhari. ***Sahih al-Bukhari***. tr. Muhammad Muhsin Khan. vol. 2, ch. 23 (New Delhi: Kitab Bhavan, India, 1987) p 232.

Attitudes Towards the Prophet Muhammad: the two extremes

Denigration, Vilification and Worse

In Karen Armstrong's book, *Muhammad: A Biography* —', a marvelous job has been done of documenting and analyzing Western attitudes toward Muhammad ﷺ. The following is a brief summary of the chapter titled "Muhammad the Enemy"[1] in her book.

The rise of Islam was a political threat, and a religious catastrophe to the Christian world of that time. Muhammad ﷺ was immediately labeled as the antichrist, the great pretender, whose reign would herald the Last Days. The prevalent view was that the antichrist would establish his rule in the temple of Jerusalem and mislead many of the Christians with plausible doctrines. In the Christian mind, Muhammad ﷺ appeared to fit the prophecy of the antichrist perfectly. In a fear-ridden fantasy, Muhammad ﷺ, was portrayed by the Christians as an impostor, a charlatan, a lecher, and Islam was portrayed as the religion of the sword. This fictional portrait of "Mahound" (synonym for devil) persisted at a popular level for a long time.[2] Islam also raised a troubling theological question for the Christians: Where was the need for Islam and how could God allow this "impious faith" to prosper when He had already given the world a chance for salvation through His grace and the vicarious atonement of Christ?

By the end of the eleventh century, as Europe was beginning to rise, the wars of *Reconquista* had begun. In 1085, Alfonso VI conquered Toledo back from the Muslims, and in 1095, Pope Urban II (1088-1099) summoned the knights of Europe to liberate the tomb of Christ in Jerusalem and proclaimed the First Crusade at the Council of Clermont. Songs written at the time of the Crusades show the depth of ignorance about Islam. Muslims were depicted as "idol worshippers," bowing down before a trinity of "Apollo (the ancient

21

Greek and roman god of prophecy, poetry, and music sometimes identified with the god of light and truth or sun), *Tervagant* (French word for a violent and overbearing fictional deity attributed to Muslims; it's English derivative termagant means quarrelsome or shrewish), and Mahomet!"

In 1099 when the Crusaders conquered Jerusalem, Muslims were brutally massacred. The official words used to describe them were "filth" and "vermin." At a time when the positive myths of King Arthur, Robin Hood, and Charlemagne were evolving in the West, the negative myth of "Mahound" the enemy was already firmly established. The creation of an evil myth may have been necessary in order to define the myth of the "noble" Christians. Walter Lippmann,[3] the notable columnist and social scientist, speculates that we tend to define "self" by first stereotyping "the other." Hence Islam became the despised reaction to benevolent Christianity. Muhammad ﷺ was claimed to have concocted miracles like that of the "white-bull," which terrorized the population and finally appeared with the Qur'an between its horns. One explanation given for the divine revelations he was receiving was that they were the result of epilepsy. Another story tells of a heretical monk named Sergius who presumably taught Muhammad ﷺ a distorted version of Christianity.

The stereotyping was not confined to Muhammad ﷺ and the Muslims. At the same time, Christians evolved terrifying fantasies about Jews who were allegedly killing children and mixing their blood with Passover bread. In fact, the first Crusaders began their journey to Jerusalem by massacring Jewish communities along the Rhine valley. In the Lateran councils in 1179 and 1215, Muslims and Jews were linked together as common enemies.[4] They were to wear distinctive clothing and not to appear on the streets during Christian festivals or hold public office. This type of early branding can be seen later in history during the Second World War.

Early in the 14th century Pope Clement V (1305-14) declared the Islamic presence on Christian soil as an insult to God inciting further waves of violence and hatred. In 1492, Ferdinand and Isabella conquered Granada and Spanish Muslims were given a choice of either conversion to Catholicism or deportation from their native land. Those who converted to Catholicism were nevertheless persecuted as crypto-Muslims for many years.

There were signs of a schizophrenic attitude towards Muslims at the time. In Dante's "*Inferno*,"[5] Ibn Sina (Avicenna) and Ibn Rushd (Averroes) are in limbo with the virtuous pagans like Euclid, Ptolemy, Socrates, Plato, and Aristotle, while Muhammad himself is in the eighth circle of the hell with the schismatics.

In the sixteenth century, Luther saw the Pope and the Catholic Church as the real enemies of true Christianity. This, according to Luther, had allowed the Christians to be open to Islam. Many of the Christians including Luther continued to see Islam as a failed version of Christianity.

At the end of the seventeenth century, and the early eighteenth century, during the Renaissance period (the age of Enlightenment), the *Bibliotheque Orientale* written by Barthelmy d'Herrbelot, appeared with the following disappointing description under the entry "Mahomet."

"This is the famous impostor Mahomet, author and founder of a heresy, which has taken on the name of religion, which we call Mohammadanism"... surely not an enlightened description of Muhammad ﷺ.

In the next century, relatively fair interpretations of Islam started appearing in the West. In 1708, Simon Ockley, the well-known English Arabist, published the first balanced book, *History of the Saracens*, that gave a just account of the history and spread of Islam. In 1734, George Sale published a fairly accurate translation of the Qur'an titled *The Koran, commonly called the Alcoran of Mohammed....* However, he appended to this translation, a highly vituperative essay titled *A Life of Mohammed*.[6] In this essay he wrote " when the character of Mohammed is attentively surveyed—it is so shocking that it is a wonder that the country of his nativity has not been buried in oblivion. Any country would have blushed to produce such a monster."

During this century, another "fantasy" about the Prophet ﷺ began to emerge. According to this new fantasy, Muhammad was a great military hero not unlike Julius Caesar and Alexander the Great, who had fabricated the religion to become the master of the world. Needless to stay it fed into the stereotype of Islam as a militant religion.

At the end of the eighteenth century, Edward Gibbon, the greatest English historian of his time and author of *The History of the Decline and Fall of the Roman Empire* (1776-1788)[7], which praised the monotheism of Islam and started giving the Muslim venture its proper place in history. Thomas Carlyle (1795-1881)[8], Scottish essayist, historian, and an influential social critic defended the Prophet ﷺ in *On Heroes, Hero-Worship, and Heroic in History*, but dismissed the Qur'an as the most "wearisome, confused jumble, crude, incondite; endless iterations, long windedness, entanglement, — insupportable stupidity in short."

The "colonial spirit," driven by a belief in racial superiority, and a mission to civilize the barbaric native inhabitants of the conquered territories, characterized the nineteenth century. During the French Revolution, Islam continued to be seen as "the opposite of us." In the Qur'an, the European authors during the French Revolution concluded, there was "neither a principle for civilization nor a mandate that can elevate character."

In the nineteenth century, Washington Irving (1783-1859), one of America's more admired writers of fiction and folklore was fascinated by Prophet Muhammad's ﷺ persona and wrote a biography of him. Irving became interested in Islam when he arrived in Spain as diplomatic representative of the U.S. during the winter of 1823. From entries in his diary we learn that Irving spent at times whole days writing the legend of "Mahomet". In 1831 he submitted a complete manuscript for publication that because of disagreements with the publisher remained unpublished until 1849.

The self-righteous, intolerant, 'Crusader mentality' of the twelfth century, which regarded Muslims as a hated enemy and Muhammad ﷺ as an impostor, continued into the twentieth century. When the British General, Edmond Allenby arrived in Jerusalem in 1917, he announced, "Now, the Crusades are over." Similarly demonstrating the animus of Christianity against Islam, the French commander Gouravd on arrival to Damascus in 1920, immediately marched to Saladin's (Sultan Salahuddin Ayyubi) tomb and cried, "*Nous revenous,* Salladin.'(We have returned O Saladin!).

Although European Christendom harbored many myths about Muhammad ﷺ, and continued to regard Muslims as their enemy, the Muslim world itself was relatively unaware of the extent of Christian prejudice and animosity toward them until just 200 years ago (the Crusades had a relatively local impact upon Muslims). After all, the Qur'an had taught the Muslims to respect the Jews and Christians as the "People of the Book". They assumed incorrectly that this sentiment would be automatically reciprocated. Initially, as the Muslims started realizing the extent of this prejudice, their feelings were mixed. There was a great admiration for Western liberalism, as well as increasing sense of dismay at being the targets of unjustified stereotyping. As the "double standards" and "selective morality" of the West became more widely evident, more recently during the political and religious conflicts in Palestine, Bosnia, Kosova and Chechnya, much of the initial goodwill towards the West was lost.

The West continues to generate new stereotypes of the Muslims, such as the oil rich sheik of the '70's, the fanatical Ayatollah of the 1980's, and the religion which kills creativity and freedom of speech (after the Rushdie affair). Some scholars continue to publish prejudicial essays and books on Muhammad ﷺ and Muslims. There is a refreshing trend, however, of a growing number of scholars who are making an honest and non-prejudicial attempt at understanding Islam. They are generally objective, fair and empathetic in their writings. These include, Louis Massignon, H.A.R. Gibb, Henri Corbin, Marshall G.S. Hodgson, William G. Milward, Wilfred Cantwell Smith, Annmarie Schimmel, Ralph Braibanti, John L Esposito, John O Voll, Yvonne Haddad, Karen Armstrong, and many others. Although they remain a minority, they represent a historically significant phenomenon.

The Other Extreme: Near Deification

As the West distorted the image of Muhammad ﷺ, it experienced a different transformation in parts of the Muslim world acquiring a cosmic status. Wilfred Cantwell Smith's observation describes quite accurately the attitude of many Muslims toward Muhammad ﷺ when he says, "Muslims will allow attacks on Allah. There are atheists, atheistic publications, and rationalistic societies. But to disparage Muhammad will provoke from even the most 'liberal' sections of the community, a reaction of blazing vehemence."⁹

The Qur'an itself is quite clear about the role of the Prophet ﷺ. He is neither a divine presence nor an angel, but a human being and a Messenger:

> —*Say: Glory to my Lord! <u>I am aught but a man, sent as a Messenger</u>*
> *(Qur'an 17: 93)*

> *They ask thee, "When is this Hour*
> *(the Day of Judgment) to happen*
> *Of which you speak so often?"*
> *(Say) Its time is known only to thy Lord*
> *<u>--thou art but a warner</u> to those who pay heed.*
> *(Qur'an 79: 42-45)*

Yet, among many works of devotional writings and poetry, the Prophet's ﷺ persona became nearly divine. The religion of Allah ﷻ (*Din* of Allah), in a way, was seemingly replaced by the religion of Muhammad ﷺ (*Din* of Muhammad). The veneration extends even to the preservation and periodic of viewing of relics like the Prophet's ﷺ hair. (For example, a well-known shrine in Kashmir is called the Hadrat Bal Masjid: Mosque of the Prophet's hair).

This excessive veneration may be understood better by a typical quote from a renowned Persian poet, Mawlana Nur ad-Din Abd ar-Rahman Jami (1414-1492).

> *The sky became curved because of prostration before Muhammad*
> *The ocean is only a water bubble from Muhammad's generosity.*
> *The moon is a reflection of Muhammad's beauty.*
> *Musk is a little whiff from Muhammad's mole and tresses.*

As Annmarie Schimmel observes with uncommon insight, this type of veneration of great religious leaders is understandable and not uncommon. She further elucidates that "the charisma of a true religious leader can be better recognized from such legends (legends crystallized around a nucleus of factual material) than from dry facts of his life."[10]

Although the love, affection, respect and loyalty for him is genuine and touching to behold, some Muslims do not realize that in their acts of excessive veneration, they come dangerously close to deification. Paradoxically, these attitudes negate both the intent of the Qur'an and Muhammad's ﷺ intent. Muhammad's ﷺ hope was that he would be remembered as the final Messenger of the Lord almighty, the Warner, the Teacher, the Exhorter and the Exemplar *par excellence*, but not someone to be hero worshipped or deified. This is a subtle but important distinction. His greatest attribute may have been that he was unafraid to be a human. He appeared to be conscious of the fact that to deify a person is to create an excuse not to emulate him or aspire to reach the standards of excellence set by that individual, thus violating the fundamental expectation that his example could be followed.

---

[1] Karen Armstrong. ***Muhammad: A Biography of the Prophet.*** (San Francisco: Harper, 1992) pp. 21-44.

[2] The modern version of this view point is found in the pronouncement of the Televangelists who propagate "biblical inerrancy' and literal belief in the biblical prophesies. For further details, consult Dewey M Beegle, ***Prophecy and Politics*** (Westford, CT: Laurence Hill, 1986), and ***Prophecy And Prediction.*** (Ann Arbor, MI: Pryor Pettingill, 1978).

[3] Walter Lippman. (Originally published 1922) ***Public Opinion.*** (New York: Free Press, 1965) p. 9 and cf. p. 57.

[4] Lateran Councils: Ecumenical councils of the Roman Catholic church, held in the Lateran Palace, Rome.

[5] Dante's epic, *The Divine Comedy,* was probably begun about 1307; it was completed shortly before his death. The work is an allegorical narrative of the poet's imaginary journey through hell, purgatory, and heaven. It is divided into three sections, correspondingly named the *Inferno* (Hell), the *Purgatorio* (Purgatory), and the *Paradiso* (Paradise). In each of these three realms the poet meets with mythological, historical, and contemporary personages. Each character is symbolic of a particular fault or virtue, either religious or political; and the punishment or rewards meted out to the characters further illustrates the way Dante understood their actions in the universal scheme. The work provides a summary of the political, scientific, and philosophical thought of the time, and is an accurate representation of medieval Christian theology and prejudices.

For a critical overview of Dante's attitude toward Islam, see Syed Hossein Nasr's "Dante and Islam", *Journal of Islamic Studies*

[6] George Sale. *The Koran: Commonly called the Alkoran of Mohammed; translated into English immediately from the original Arabic, with explanatory notes ... to which is prefixed A Life Of Mohammed.* (New York: A.L.Burt Company, 1734) pp. 1-49.

[7] Edward Gibbon (1737-1794), the greatest English historian of his time and author of *The History of the Decline and Fall of the Roman Empire* (1776-1788).

[8] Thomas Carlyle (1795-1881), Scottish essayist and historian, who was an influential social critic. In one of his essays titled, "On Heroes, Hero-Worship, and the Heroic in History" (1841), he contended that world civilization had developed because of the activities of heroes.

[9] Wilfred Cantwell Smith. *Modern Islam in India.* (Lahore: 1947) p. 69-70.

[10] *Ibid.* p. 9.

Chapter 1

The Search for Light in a Period of Darkness

*And relieved thee of the burden
which had weighed down thy back...*
(Qur'an 94:2-3)

Chapter I: the Search for Light in a Period of Darkness

The Seeker of Truth

The purpose of this article is not to review world history at the time of the advent of Islam, therefore my comments here are necessarily broad and sweeping in character. The seventh century appears to have been a time of world wide moral confusion and decay. Christianity had divided into various factions and controversies surrounded the personalities of Jesus ﷷ and his mother, Mary. The Roman Catholic and Eastern Orthodox churches exhibited deep prejudice and intolerance against each other. In Persia, absolutism of the monarchical system influenced and controlled most aspects of the society. Zoroastrianism was also unraveling. In addition to the internal turmoil, Christianity and Zoroastrianism were in a constant state of friction. India and China were similarly morally adrift. India had thrown out Buddhism out of its birth land, and the old polytheistic practices were resurgent. The oppressive caste system, which Buddhism had revolted against, was as entrenched as ever. In China, at the same time as a great flowering of the arts, music and dance was occurring, there was a general sense of moral confusion. Many Chinese individuals claimed to be the followers of all of the three prevailing traditions: Confucianism, Taoism, and Buddhism. Buddha had been turned into an object of worship and huge statues depicting his likeness were commonplace. This was a surprising turn of events for a non-theistic religion whose founder had never claimed divinity, or prescribed idol worship.

The Arabian Peninsula, with the exception of Yemen, which was on the caravan route, was in darkness. Little was known about it to the outside world. Polytheism and idol worship were rampant in Arabia, as was tribalism and unrestrained pursuit of wealth and power. Most Arabs were nomads, who felt assured by tribal security. This stability was based largely on the tradition of "blood vengeance," which invariably resulted in an endless cycle of revenge. Society seemed even harsher in the cities. At the time, there were only a few cities like

Makkah, Yathrib (later *Madinat an-Nabi*, 'City of the Prophet' or for short Madinah), and Ta'if. A small number of rich and powerful families controlled the economy. Many of the poor were eternally entangled in a web of usury *riba*. This system of *riba* turned them into virtual slaves. Slavery itself was commonplace. Women's status was also extremely deplorable and they were treated largely as chattel, which was essentially another form of slavery. Marriage, inheritance, and divorce laws reflected the chauvinistic attitudes prevalent in the society. For example, unlimited polygamy was widespread; primogeniture was the rule and sons often inherited their fathers' wives. A husband could stop conjugal relations with his wife and abdicate all responsibilities toward her without divorcing her and letting her go free. This cruel treatment of wives called *zihar* (turning your back on something) was widely practiced.

Although females were oppressed and abused routinely (female infanticide was commonplace, and male progeny was a source of pride and status in society), the majority of deities were female. The three major deities, al-Lat, al-'Uzza, and al-Manat were considered the daughters of Allah.

Have you seen al-Lat and al-Uzza and the third Manat?
What for you the male gender and for Him the female!
(Qur'an 53:19-21)

The Qur'an refers to the practice of burying alive infant girls by posing this poignant question;

When the female infant buried alive
will ask for what crime was she killed?
(Qur'an 81:8-9)

These injustices, inequities, and cruelties weighed heavily on the shoulders of at least some of the individuals living in Arabia. In spite of rampant polytheism and idol worship, some did have a concept of a transcendent God whom they called Allah.[1]

The Qur'an refers to this in the following verses:

Chapter I: the Search for Light in a Period of Darkness

If indeed thou ask them who has created the heavens the earth and subjected the sun and the moon (to His law), they will certainly reply, Allah.
How are they then led away (from the truth)?
Allah enlarges the sustenance (which He gives) to whichever of His servants He pleases;

And if indeed thou ask them who it is that sends down rain from the sky,
And gives life therewith to the earth after its death, they will certainly reply, Allah!
But most of them understand not.

What is the life of this world but amusement and play?
But verily the home in the Hereafter -
that is life indeed, if they but knew
Now if they embark on a boat they call on Allah, making their devotion sincerely to Him.
But when He has delivered them safely to land behold they give a share of their worship to others!
(Qur'an 29: 61-65)

Ibn Ishaq records that there were at least four individuals in Makkah who had turned away from idol worship and polytheism and had adopted the monotheism of Prophet Ibrahim ﷺ (Abraham). Amongst them was included the important figure, Waraqah bin Nawfal, who later verified the authenticity of Muhammad's ﷺ Prophethood. These people were called the Hanifs (the upright men or those who turn away [from idol worship]).²

Born in 570 C.E. Muhammad ﷺ was orphaned early in his life and was raised initially by a loving but poor grandfather, Abd al-Muttalib, and later by his uncle Abu Talib. In these early years, Muhammad ﷺ emerges as a quiet, thoughtful and introspective individual. He earned a reputation for being trustworthy (*al-Amin*), diplomatic and wise. There was an incident in his youth, during the rebuilding of the Ka'bah, when a dispute arose over which tribe should place the "Black Stone" *(al-Hajar al-Aswad)* back in its previous spot. Muhammad ﷺ solved the problem by placing the stone on his cloak and asked members of all the tribes to lift it up. He then laid the stone in its designated spot himself.

He proved himself a conscientious and successful businessperson and caravan leader. This business acumen and his widely known reputation of trustworthiness, thoughtfulness and gentility attracted the attention of Khadijah. An exceptional woman, Khadijah was a prominent businesswoman in a misogynist society. She had been married twice before and was a widow. Her marriage to Muhammad ﷺ was very fruitful and lasted until the rest of her life. They had six children, two sons who died as infants) and four daughters (Zaynab, Ruqayyah, Umm kulthum and Fatima).

Although married to a wealthy woman, the Prophet ﷺ continued to lead a frugal life and spent much time in meditation. His favorite place for meditation was the Hira cave about three miles from Makkah. He would spend the entire month of Ramadan (the ninth month of the lunar calendar, and later the month during which Muslims were ordained to fast in order to practice abstinence and self-discipline to attain personal piety) meditating in this cave. This practice of meditating in seclusion, striving for wisdom and righteousness was common among the Arabs and was called "*Tahannuf*." The cave of Hira was where he received his initial revelation. However after he received the first revelation, which was in essence a call for action, the Prophet ﷺ never went back to the cave.

It is difficult to resist drawing analogies between the seventh century world and the state of the human morality in today's world at the turn of the new millennium. The nuclear man-woman, two-parent family, as a core unit of society has eroded seriously in the West. Brazen sexual exploitation in the media is commonplace and illicit sex condoned and even accepted. Violence at home, against women, children, and violence in the streets, is frightfully routine. Substance abuse is widespread, with United States as the largest consumer of drugs in the world. Alcoholism is rampant, especially among college students, with only feeble attempts being made to address the problem. The lessons from the AIDS epidemic are being swept under the rug of political correctness. African-Americans have been liberated as slaves for a century and a half, yet many are still trapped in an unending cycle of poverty and discrimination, which is a form of economic slavery. Because of a system that allows unrestrained growth of wealth without encouraging proper redistribution, economic disparities and injustices continue to grow at an alarming rate.

However, there are many excellent characteristics in Western societies, especially in the US, particularly freedom of thought, speech and assembly, a tolerant attitude toward eccentricities in human nature and an ambition to be a just and compassionate society. Many of these qualities, especially freedom of speech, thought and pluralism, are sadly lacking in many Muslim societies. Nevertheless, the moral and socio-economic scene of today's world is uncannily similar to seventh century Arabia before the advent of Islam.

The unraveling of the moral fabric in today's society must weigh heavily on the minds of individuals with insight. They can draw personal solace and inspiration from the Prophet's ﷺ life. The Arab tribal society of the seventh century, whose structure was based on greed, debauchery, and violence, was changed in a very short time, by the Prophet ﷺ, into a society with one of the highest moral standards in history. Compassion, humility, devotion to God and egalitarianism replaced the old well-entrenched tribal attitudes of pride in wealth, family and class, cruelty toward fellow humans and self-centered behavior. Women, for the first time in history, had rights and dignity, and the vulnerable and weak sections of the society were protected. Sexuality was removed from public prurience and became private and wholesome. Wealth was re-circulated so that even the smallest capillaries of the society were infused with energy and indigence became nearly extinct.

Those who are receptive to learning from Muhammad's ﷺ mission can draw inspiration and hope to reform society. Their biggest challenge will be to grasp the core values of his message by removing the accretions of cultural practices, vagaries of time and historical events that have confounded it. They cannot turn to any of the modern Muslim nations to search for paradigms of Muhammad's ﷺ community during his life. In fact in many Muslim countries and communities, anthropologists and social scientists discern the perplexing paradox of rapidly increasing enthusiasm for Islam and respect for Muhammad ﷺ, and the persistence of very high levels of corruption, tribalism, violence, intolerance and injustice, which are the antithesis of the very ideals which he preached and practiced in his life.

If the thoughtful analyst is successful in this attempt at understanding the core values of the Prophet's ﷺ message, then he is likely to come up with dynamic and innovative solutions to current and future problems. The approach by most Muslims at solving current problems has been imitative rather than innovative.[3] The lessons that the analyst obtains are likely to have universal value and applicability, as human needs and problems are essentially the same regardless of color, ethnicity, race, religion or the millennium in which the person is living.

---

[1] The use of the word Allah by the pre Islamic Arabs did not imply a monotheistic philosophy. Rather it referred to one superior God in panoply of multiple Gods. It is very similar to the *Param Ishwara* or the God of Gods concept in Hinduism. Nevertheless it is important to note that the word Allah itself was in common usage before the advent of Islam.

[2] Alfred Guillame. ***The Life of Muhammad: A Translation of Ibn Ishaq's "Sirat Rasul Allah"***. (Oxford: Oxford University Press, 1982) pp. 98-100.

[3] An excellent discussion of this issue may be found in Abdul Hamid A. Abu Sulayman's book ***The Crisis in the Muslim Mind***. 1st ed. (Herndon, Virginia: International Institute Of Islamic Thought, 1993).

Chapter II

The Revelation (Wahy) and Its Immediate Aftermath

Recite in the name of Allah Who created...
(Qur'an 96:1)

The Seven Phases of Prophet Muhammad's Life

Chapter II: the Revelation and Its Immediate Aftermath

The Recipient of the Mantle of Messengerhood, The Warner and Exhorter

The first revelation (*Wahy*) in the cave of Hira marked the beginning of Islam. The instrument of (*Wahy*) continued to be the primary source of guidance he received over the next twenty-three years.

> *It is not in man's power that Allah*
> *should converse (directly) with him*
> *except by means of <u>Revelation (Wahy)</u>*
> *Or from behind a veil,*
> *Or by His permission,*
> *He sends a Messenger (Angel Gabriel)*
> *to reveal what He will:*
> *For He is supremely wise.*
> *(Qur'an 42:51)*

The (*Wahy)* took many forms. The Prophet ﷺ reported, "Revelation sometimes comes like the sound of a bell; that is the most painful way. When it ceases, I have remembered what was said. Sometimes it is an angel who talks to me like a human, and I remember what he says."[1]

The words he heard during that first revelation in the cave have been immortalized in the Qur'an.

> *Iqra' (Recite) in the name of your Lord*
> *(The Nourisher and Sustainer),*
> *Who has created (all things)*
> *He has created humankind from a clot (fetus)*
> *Recite! And your Lord is the most generous*
> *<u>Who has taught (mankind) by the pen</u>*
> *He taught humankind what he knew not*
> *(Qur'an 96:1-4)*

It is clear that for the Prophet ﷺ the *Wahy* was an awe-inspiring experience. He felt physically crushed by it and was emotionally overpowered by the weight and majesty of the message as it sank into his psyche.

The words that Khadijah used to reassure Muhammad ﷺ when he went home after the first revelation, obviously shaken by the experience, are particularly insightful. When Muhammad ﷺ cried out in anguish, "Woe, have I become a poet or am I possessed?" Khadijah answered, "Allah will never disgrace you thus. You keep good relations with your kith and kin, help the poor and the destitute, serve your guests generously and assist those afflicted by calamity."[2]

With this first revelation in 610 CE, at forty years of age, the second phase in Muhammad's ﷺ life began, a phase of private preaching of Islam. Along with this discreet spread of Islam came hardship, and continuing self-doubt and need for reassurance.

Muhammad's ﷺ doubts about the nature of what was happening to him must have been exacerbated during a long period (six months to two years called *fatrah* or break) without any revelation. In addition there must have been a sense of absolute loneliness. Any individual who sets out with a vision that is truly unique will be predictably lonely in the beginning. It is the very uniqueness of the mission, which makes one lonely. Frequently, the individual is the victim of derision, sarcasm, and jest. Most charismatic leaders have had to go through this phase of loneliness, uncertainty and sometimes depression.

Approximately six months after the initial revelation came the following exhortation to pray and a warning of the profound and difficult nature of the message he was to receive.

O thou enfolded in thy mantle
Keep awake in the night, but for a portion of it-
a half of it or less
Or a little more than that;
and intone the Qur'an in measured tone
<u>We shall charge thee with a weighty message</u>.
(Qur'an 73:1-5)

Khadijah had instantly accepted the divine nature of the revelation. A small number of Quraysh followed suit surreptitiously. The most influential among those who accepted Islam early on was Abu Bakr . He was typical in many ways of those who tended to accept Islam. He was serious-minded, thoughtful, and given to introspection—someone who had already been searching for the truth. Some of the others who accepted Islam were from the group mentioned earlier called the *Hanifs.*

Muhammad ﷺ also started praying using physical postures quite different from the prevalent Qurayshi methods. Initially the prayers were offered in the privacy of homes or in secluded spots. Once one of Muhammad's ﷺ uncles accidentally stumbled upon Ali who was in the act of prayer. Somewhat puzzled at the unfamiliar activity, he wondered what was going on, to which Ali ibn Abu Talib replied that he had been taught by Muhammad ﷺ to pray according to the rituals of Ibrahim, a figure who was well known to the Arabs. The tendency in Islam toward finding commonalties with Judaism and Christianity through their shared Abrahamic (Ibrahimi) tradition was present from the very beginning. As mentioned earlier, Christians and Jews are referred to in the Qur'an by the phrase, *Ahl al-Kitab* (the people of the book) which gives them a special and higher status than the followers of other religions.

Excitement and Self Doubt

It seems Muhammad's ﷺ overwhelming sense of these first three years after the revelation is of awe at the majesty of the revelation, a great sense of excitement, but also of torturous self-doubt. The Qur'an alludes to this and consoles Muhammad ﷺ in the poignant *Surat ad-Duha* (The Glorious Morning Light),

By the glorious morning light,
And by the night when it is still,
<u>Thy Lord has not forsaken thee, nor is he displeased.</u>
<u>Verily the end will be better for thee than the present.</u>
And soon will thy Lord give thee

> *that which will please thee.*
> *Did he not find thee an orphan and give thee shelter.*
> *And found thee wandering (lost) and give thee guidance.*
> *And found thee destitute (in need)*
> *and made thee independent.*
> *(Qur'an 93: 1-8)*

The hope and promise of a future as glorious as the morning light after a dark night suffuses and illuminates both this and the following surah, "The Broadening" in which the Qur'an reminds Muhammad ﷺ that,

> *There is ease after each difficulty,*
> *Indeed ease after each difficulty.*
> *(Qur'an 94: 5-6)*

The first three years after the initial revelation were ending. The early doubts had finally melted away. There was a small but dedicated group of believers and the time appeared to be ripe for taking the message to the public.

> *Therefore expound <u>openly</u> what thou art commanded...*
> *And turn away from those who join false gods with Allah.*
> *(Qur'an 15: 94)*

There was also the order to spread the message to one's close relatives.

> *And admonish your nearest kinsmen.*
> *(Qur'an 26: 214)*

And hence these trepidations of the first few years came to an end and the next phase of his life started, which was marked by a more open style of invitation to Islam and a concomitant increase in hostility and resistance from his opponents. It is both fascinating and revealing that even the individual who would later be rated as the most influential man in human history had these initial periods of doubt and uncertainty about his mission. It was the reassurance from the Qur'an and the confidence and support of his wife Khadijah, and his close companions which provided him the support that he needed-surely a lesson for us lesser mortals!

---

[1] *al-Bukhari*. tr. Muhammad Muhsin Khan. (New Delhi: Kitab Bhavan, 1987) vol 1, ch. 1: *Bab al-Wahy* (The Book of Revelation) vol. 2, p. 2.

[2] *Ibid.* vol 3. p. 4.

Chapter III

Open Invitation and Brazen Hostility

*Know then that I am the bearer of good tidings
and a warner...*
(Sirah Ibn Hisham)

Chapter III: Open Invitation and Brazen Hostility

The Stoic Optimist

Muhammad's ﷺ first attempt at public invitation (*da'wah*) was when he climbed atop a hill near Makkah and addressed the gathering, "O! the people of Quraysh. If I were to tell you that I see a cavalry on the other side of the mountain, would you believe me?" When they answered in the affirmative, he said, "Know then that I am a warner and that I warn you of a severe punishment... unless you affirm that there is no God but Allah." Though Muhammad's ﷺ plea had a sense of urgency, the Quraysh decisively rebuffed him.

Muhammad's ﷺ second effort at proselytization was to his relatives and tribe at a banquet he gave at his home. This invitation also was ignored. Ali [1], who was then merely a boy, was the only exception and offered to be Muhammad's ﷺ helper, incurring the derision of those present at the meal.

Although neither of the two invitations had a significant immediate effect, the word spread. Hardly a day would pass by without someone joining the fold of Islam. The Quraysh became increasingly alarmed at this trend. The new religion posed a great threat to the hegemony of the Quraysh over Makkah. The Quraysh held the honor of being the social and religious leaders of the Arabs. Their family was sometimes called the "family of Allah," or "Allah's neighbors", and held all the important positions which had to do with administration of the Ka'bah and performing of the rituals within it.

Another reason why the Quraysh were opposed to Islam was envy. The Quraysh could not reconcile themselves to the fact that a poor orphan was the recipient of the revelation and not one of their rich and powerful leaders. Envy and ignorance have always been the root cause of stereotyping and blind hatred.[2],[3]

Also they say, Why is not the Qur'an sent down to some leading man, in either of the two cities?
(Qur'an 43:31)

They also looked down upon Muhammad ﷺ because he did not have a surviving male progeny, since both his sons from Khadijah died before they were two years old.

The most important reason, though, was that the morality which Islam was advocating in its oft repeated dictum, "Believe and live righteously,"[4] was a direct attack on the lifestyle of the rich and powerful in the community. The challenge which Muhammad ﷺ presented, as Hodgson points out in his book *The Venture Of Islam* was to "rise to a level of personal moral piety such as had occurred to few to dream of. He (Muhammad ﷺ) presented it as a real possibility for human beings. He presented it in a concrete, tangible form in which, by an act of will, they could adopt a new ideal practically".[5] In a society where pride and conceit, lying and deceit, sexual decadence and mindless cruelty were the norm of the day, and compassion and mercy were looked down upon as character flaws. The Qur'an's challenge of building up morality and changing long entrenched personal behavior proved to be both threatening and infuriating to many of the prominent leaders of Makkah.

In spite of their anger and frustration, the Makkans were leery of physically harming Muhammad ﷺ. As he was under the protection of the tribe of Banu Hashim, killing Muhammad ﷺ would start the tribal cycle of revenge killing which could go on *ad infinitum*. Moreover as the total number of Muslims at that time was only about forty to fifty, Muhammad ﷺ was not considered a serious threat. This, however, did not prevent the Quraysh from plotting against him constantly. Qur'an talks about one such individual, who was prominent in opposition to Muhammad ﷺ. (Some exegetes believe this individual was Walid ibn Mughayrah.)

For he thought (and) he plotted
And woe to him how he plotted
Yea woe to him how he plotted
Then he looked around, Then he frowned and he scowled
Then he turned back and was haughty
Then said he "this (Qur'an) is nothing but magic
This is nothing but the word of a mortal."
(Qur'an 74: 18-26)

Chapter III: Open Invitation and Brazen Hostility

As part of a campaign to destroy his credibility, Muhammad ﷺ was maligned as a poet, a soothsayer, and a possessed man.

So go on with thy mission (O Prophet)
for thou art not by the favor of thy Lord
either a sooth-sayer or one possessed.
(Qur'an 52: 29 - 30)

I swear by the stars and their rising and setting,
And by the night as it falleth,
And by the dawn as it brighteneth.
This is verily the word of an apostle,
gracious by nature, endowed with wisdom
emanating from the Lord of the Throne:
Deserving of obedience and trust.
And your compatriot is not possessed.
(Qur'an 81:15-22)

The Quraysh would frequently dump filth and garbage on Muhammad ﷺ and spread thorns in his path. It is fascinating to note how stoic and patient Muhammad's ﷺ response was to these types of provocation. Once when he noticed that the woman who would routinely thrown thorns in his path had not done so, he went over to inquire if she had become ill.

The poor and unprotected among the Muslims, especially the slaves, were brutally tortured. One notable example was the torture of Bilal. Every time pain was inflicted on him, his response, referring to Allah ﷻ, was "*Ahad*" (One and only One). Some of these Muslims succumbed to this physical abuse. It is indeed extraordinary that these early followers of Muhammad ﷺ were so steadfast in their beliefs that they would endure this torment sometimes until it proved fatal. It is worth noting that by then, only a small portion of the Qur'an had been revealed. This was before the battle of Badr and other victories, which means that none of these early converts knew if Islam would survive as a religion.

Another tactic that the Quraysh employed to attempt to modulate Muhammad's ﷺ behavior was bribery. This prompted the famous retort by Muhammad ﷺ, which is recorded by

Haykal, "By Allah, if even they place the sun in one hand and the moon in my other hand, I will not be dissuaded from my mission."[6]

One benefit of Muhammad's ﷺ incessant public humiliation and his patient acceptance of it, was the conversion to Islam of Hamzah bin Abdul Muttalib. Hamzah a prominent and powerful individual in Makkah could not stand to see his cousin being abused any longer. Within a few days of Hamzah's acceptance of Islam, Umar Ibn al-Khattab, who would become the second Khalifah (Caliph) of Islam, also became a Muslim. Initially angered by his sister and brother-in-law's becoming Muslim, 'Umar was quickly metamorphosed when he heard the following verses:

Whatever is in the heavens and on earth,
Let it declare the praises of Allah,
For He is the exalted in might, the Wise,
To Him belongs the dominion of the heavens and the earth,
It is He who gives Life and Death, and He has power over all things...
(Qur'an 57:1-5)

He had never heard anything as eloquent, compelling and majestic as these verses.

Migration to Abyssinia (Ethiopia) of Some Muslims (the First Hijrah)

The continuous persecution lead to the first migration of Muslims to Abyssinia (modern Ethiopia). This occurred in the fifth year of the revelation. Fifteen individuals, eleven men and four women, were in the group, which traveled on a merchant ship to Abyssinia. The objective was not merely escaping persecution. It appears to have been at least partly an attempt to spread Islam. In fact, some of the most persecuted Muslims like Bilal, 'Amr and Yasir did not migrate. Amongst those who migrated were prominent people like Uthman ibn 'Affan who was clearly not at risk of being persecuted. Abyssinia may have been chosen as a country to mi-

Chapter III: Open Invitation and Brazen Hostility

grate to as the Christian king Negus, who was known for his tolerance and generosity, ruled it. In addition, Muslims felt more empathetic to Christians than to any other contemporary religious group because of the commonalties between the two religions.

The Quraysh decided to pursue the Muslims vigorously and make an example out of them. They petitioned Negus for the Muslims' repatriation back to Makkah. This lead to a court appearance by the Muslims who had a dramatic dialogue with Negus.[7] When Negus asked, "What is this new religion which is against both idol worship and Christianity?" Ja'far ibn Abi Talib (Ali's brother), replied in part, "...We were ignorant, we would worship idols, eat carrion, indulge in every possible indecency. We would be cruel to our neighbors and relatives and would oppress each other and the strong would exploit the weak. Amongst us was born someone whose truthfulness and reliability became widely known. He invited us to Islam and urged us to give up idol worship, be truthful, stop being bloodthirsty, stop usurping the orphan's wealth and property, provide help to our neighbors, stop calumny against pious women, establish regular worship, practice abstinence, and give charity..."

When the Quraysh saw how impressed Negus was by this statement, they played their ultimate card. They tried to incite Negus, a good Christian, by stating that Islam was disrespectful to Christ ('Isa ﷺ). Negus challenged the Muslims to recite what the Qur'an said about 'Isa ﷺ. Ja'far ibn Abi Talib recited a few verses from *Surat Maryam* (Mary):

Thereupon, she made a sign towards him (the newborn baby Jesus, suggesting that they should speak to him rather than to her).
They said, "How shall we speak with one who is in the cradle, a mere infant?"
The babe said, "Verily, I am the servant of Allah;
He hath given me the Book, and hath made me a Prophet.
And he hath made me blessed wherever I be,
and enjoined on me regular prayer,
and alms as long as I live,
and to be duteous to my mother;

And He hath not made me to be overbearing, or depraved.
<u>*And blessed I am the day I was born*</u>
<u>*and the day I shall die,*</u>
<u>*and the day I shall be raised to life.*</u>"
(Qur'an 19:29-33)

The eloquence of the verses deeply moved Negus and his court and won the Muslims a safe stay in Abyssinia. Over the next few years, approximately eighty-three Muslims migrated to Abyssinia. Many of them returned to Makkah when they heard a rumor that the pagans of Quraysh had accepted Islam. The rumor is linked incorrectly to the infamous and fictitious incident of the satanic verses (see appendix).

Siege in Abu Talib's tribal abode (Boycott By Makkans of Muhammad's Clan)

In spite of all the hostility of the Quraysh the number of Muslims kept increasing slowly. The Quraysh in the seventh year of the mission decided to try a different tactic to stop the spread of Islam. To stop Muslim contact with the outside world they physically isolated Muhammad ﷺ, his followers and his uncle Abu Talib's tribe in the part of Makkah where they had their homes. They cut off food supplies to the clan and shut down trade and all social contact with its members. The Quraysh declared that this siege would go on, the Quraysh declared, until the tribe rescinded their protection of Muhammad ﷺ and handed him over to be punished.

This siege lasted for three long years and must have at times appeared endless and hopeless, but eventually, many of the less militant elders in Makkah could not stand to witness the misery of Abu Talib's clan any longer. The steadfast support shown to Muhammad ﷺ by his clan must have impressed them and so they decided to remove the sanctions.

Reconfirmation of the mission and rejuvenation of hope (Isra'/Mi'raj)

It was now ten years after the revelation and the ordeal of the siege was over. However the attempts at spreading the message of Islam and gaining new converts were advancing at a very slow pace. It was in this period of darkness and despondency that Muhammad ﷺ had the experience of the night journey (*Isra'*) and of the ascent through the heavens *(Mi'raj)*.

> *Glory be to Him who <u>conducted His servant by the night</u>*
> *from the holy mosque (in Makkah)*
> *to the distant mosque of al- Aqsa (in Jerusalem)*
> *The precincts of which We have hallowed that We might*
> *show him a few of our signs*
> *Verily He is all hearing all seeing.*
> *(Qur'an 17:1)*

Whether the experience was physical or spiritual is immaterial.[8] It is, however, relevant that it renewed Muhammad's ﷺ confidence in his mission and restored his sense of hope. The limits of time and space disappeared and he could perceive the unifying and eternal nature of the message of Islam. The entire universe was gathered up and laid out before his eyes and the continuity of the message and its finality were reaffirmed. The morning following this profoundly mystical event, it was reported that his face was radiant with joy.

This event did not end the years of anguish. Soon, (possibly in the year 619 C.E) two of Muhammad's ﷺ most important supporters, his uncle Abu Talib and his wife Khadijah died. The Messenger ﷺ would remember it as the "Year of Grief". With their deaths, an exponential increase in physical hardship and humiliation was heaped upon Muhammad.

Hoping to find a friendlier audience elsewhere Muhammad ﷺ made a trip to the city of Ta'if. There he ran up against the hostility of the local tribal leaders. They incited the rabble in the streets to taunt him and throw stones at him, forcing him to seek refuge in a vineyard. The prophet Muhammad ﷺ turned to his Lord in despair and pleaded:

> *O Allah,*
> *To Thee I complain of my weakness, my lack of resources and my lowliness before men.*
> *O most Merciful! Thou art the Lord of the*

weak and Thou art my Lord.
To whom wilt Thou relinquish my fate!
To one who will misuse me?
Or to an enemy to whom Thou hast given power over me?
If Thou art angry with me then I care not what happens to me.
Thy favor is all that counts for me.
I take refuge in the light of Thy countenance, by which all darkness is illuminated.
And the things of this world and next are rightly ordered.
I wish to please Thee until Thou art pleased.
There is no power and no might save in Thee.

Muhammad's ﷺ return to Makkah from Ta'if was impossible without the renewal of tribal protection. Muhammad ﷺ asked and received protection from a non-Muslim man named Mut'im bin 'Adi. This surely must have been one of the grimmest periods of Muhammad's ﷺ mission, as nothing seemed to be going right. Two of the most important people in his life had passed away. The hostility of the tribes appeared to be reaching new crescendos all the time. Attempts to invite outside tribes appeared to be fruitless as well. The difficult period when Muhammad's ﷺ mission seemed to run into a series of dead ends had reached its lowest point. He did not know that the long tunnel of despair was about to end and his mission would enter the next phase. This phase culminated in the migration to Madinah.

The patience and stoicism Muhammad ﷺ displayed during this phase has been a source of strength to many a Muslim who has found himself beleaguered by apparently hopeless circumstances.

The Prophet's ﷺ interactions with non-Muslims

'Mut'im bin 'Adi, Muhammad's ﷺ "protector" on his return from Ta'if to Makkah, was one of many non-Muslims who helped Muhammad ﷺ during his mission.

Abu Talib, his uncle and mentor, never accepted Islam,

but he remained a steadfast supporter all his life. He was the Prophet's ﷺ main protection against the wrath of the other Qurayshi clans. He and his clan suffered a great deal because of this, which included the boycott and the siege they endured for several long months. Due to the fear of retaliation and reprisal, which would be unleashed under the tribal traditions, the Quraysh were restrained from inflicting significant bodily harm to Muhammad ﷺ, as long as Abu Talib was alive. During the siege, some Quraysh smuggled in small amounts of food. The biographers record Hakim bin Hazam[9] as one who was caught by Abu Jahl while smuggling flour to the Prophet's ﷺ household.

Early in his mission, the Prophet ﷺ realized that although he was protected by his relationship with Abu Talib, many of his companions were not. They were being subjected to torture. He advised his followers to migrate to the Christian nation of Abyssinia. "If you were to go to Abyssinia (it would be better for you) for the king will not tolerate injustice and it is a friendly country" he said "until Allah shall relieve you from your distress."[10]

Another outstanding figure in the early history of Islam is the Christian elder Waraqah bin Nawfal, who may have become a Hanif[11] at the time Muhammad ﷺ received his first revelation. He listened to the description of the revelatory experience and confirmed it to be a true event rather than the hallucination of a man possessed. This was a crucial source of reassurance for Muhammad ﷺ at that time.

During the migration, the Prophet ﷺ and Abu Bakr hired Abdullah bin Arqat, a polytheist, to guide them to Madinah. They confided to him their plan to migrate, handing over two camels that Abu Bakr had prepared for the journey, and described the location of the cave where they would hide until the pursuit abated. After three days, Abdullah bin Arqat joined them with his own camel and led them safely to Madinah.

The most remarkable and the least known of these non-Muslim helpers was a Jewish Rabbi who fought along with the Muslims and died in the battle of Uhud. Ibn Hisham records his name as Mukhayriq[12] and identifies his tribe as the Banu Tha'lah. His tribesmen tried to dissuade Mukhayriq from joining the Muslims in this war by pointing out that as the battle was being fought on a Saturday, the day of Jewish Sabbath, he had a religious excuse not to participate. Mukhayriq argued that the covenant Jews and taken with the Muslims took precedence over any excuses.

When the Prophet ﷺ was forced to go out of Makkah to face the tribe of Hawazain in the battle of Hunain, he was short of weapons. He asked the wealthy polytheist Safwan bin Umayya if he would loan his weapons to the Muslims. Safwan bin Umayya wanted to know if the Prophet ﷺ was demanding them by force. The Prophet ﷺ replied that they were to be a "loan and a trust until we return them to you."[13] The Muslims borrowed a hundred coats of mail and arms.

The Prophet ﷺ continued this practice of cooperating with non-Muslims and finding common ground with them all of his life. His invitation to the rulers of the neighboring kingdoms is another example which will be discussed later in this manuscript.

Muslims these days would be well served to keep these examples in mind. The Prophet's ﷺ attitude was in perfect harmony with what the Qur'an itself says about non-Muslims.

Yet they are not all alike.
Among the people of the book an upright section
recite the word of God during the night hours
and bend in adoration.
They believe in God and the Day-After, enjoin the right,
forbid the wrong, and are eager to do good.
These are the righteous.
In addition, whatever good they do shall
by no means go unacknowledged and
Allah knoweth those who are righteous.
(Qur'an. 3: 113-115)

On another occasion in the same chapter the Qur'an says,

Among the people of the book are some
to any of whom if thou should entrust a large treasure,
he will restore it to thee;
and among them also are some

Chapter III: Open Invitation and Brazen Hostility

to anyone of who if thou shouldst give even a single dinar, he will not restore it to thee unless thou art pressing in thy demand on him.
This because they say, "We owe no responsibility to keep faith with those who have no knowledge of the Jewish scriptures," and thus they foist a lie on Allah and they do it knowingly.
(Qur'an 3: 75)

There is a tendency among some Muslims to look at all non-Muslims as enemies. That clearly wasn't the case then nor is it the case now. The list of people who empathize with the Muslim cause and have taken a courageous and noble stand on their behalf is long and impressive. The Prophet ﷺ did not have any close confidants that were non-Muslims, but he sometimes took non-Muslims into confidence in matters of extreme importance.

---

[1] Ali later became the Prophet's ﷺ son-in-law and the fourth *Khalifah* of Islam. Among Shi'i Muslims he is revered as the second most holy figure after Muhammad.

[2] John E Woods. "Imagining and Stereotyping Islam". **Muslims in America: Opportunities And Challenges**, by Asad Husain, John E Woods and Javeed Akhter. (Chicago, IL: International Strategy and Policy Institute) pp. 45-77.

[3] Even today examples of this can be seen in the attitude of some non-Muslims toward Islam. French paranoia about Hijab, the West's fear of having a potentially Muslim state of Bosnia in Europe, hatred of Muslims by many Hindus in India, and the pervasive stereotyping of Muslims by the Western media are some notable examples.

[4] The phrase "*Aminu wa' amilu as-salihat*", "believe and do righteous works", occurs many times in the Qur'an. It hammers home the crucial concept of piety in Islam that requires both beliefs in the core values of the faith and social activism to establish a just society.

[5] Marshall G.S Hodgson. ***The Venture Of Islam.*** (Chicago: The University of Chicago Press, 1977) vol. 1, p. 167.

[6] Muhammad Husayn Haykal. ***The Life of Muhammad.*** tr. Isma'il Raji al-Faruqi. (Indianapolis, Indiana: North American Trust Publications, 1976) p. 89.

[7] Guillame, ***The Life***, p. 151.

[8] Haykal, ***Life of Muhammad,*** pp. 139-147. (Haykal has a comprehensive discussion and analysis of the various points of view surrounding the Isra'/Mi'raj events.)

[9] Guillame, ***The Life***, p 160.

[10] *Ibid*, p. 146.

[11] For definition of *Hanif*, see the first section of the book, p. 41.

[12] Ibn Hisham. *Sira of the Prophet.* tr. (Urdu) Abdul Jalil Sidiqi. (Pakistan: Ghulam Ali Lahore) vol. 2, p. 72.

[13] Guillame, ***The Life***, p. 567.

Chapter IV

Unexpected Avenue for Expansion: Hijrah

*So that the conduct among believers is based
on equity and justice
(Sirah Ibn Hisham)*

Chapter IV: Unexpected Avenue for Expansion: Hijrah

The Pluralistic Leader

Yathrib (later called *Madinat an-Nabi,* the city of the Prophet ﷺ, and for short, al-Madinah) was an old city, the second largest in Arabia. Its population consisted mostly of two large Arab tribes and a number of Jewish tribes who lived in small forts around the city. The two Arab tribes, which later became the "Ansars " (helpers), were the Aws and Khazraj. The political fortunes of the two Arab tribes and the Jews of Madinah waxed and waned. Sometimes they were allies, but there was always covert and sometimes overt hostility. The Aws and Khazraj had been weakened by internecine warfare, leaving the Jewish tribes as the ascendant group.

Contact with Madinans: Oaths of Aqabah

Because of their familiarity with Judaism, the Madinan Arabs were conversant with the concept of monotheism. Since the Jewish tribes held messianic expectations, the concept of a new Prophet was not alien either. During the Hajj, Muhammad ﷺ used to go to the various tribal groups who were visiting Makkah and personally convey the message of Islam to them. This practice brought him in touch with the Madinan tribes who later were called the Ansar (Helpers). In the tenth year of his prophethood, he took his message to visitors from the Madinan tribe of Khazraj . The Qur'anic verses impressed the six to eight individuals in this group, convincing them that Muhammad was the Messiah whom the Jews of Madinah seemed to be awaiting. They wanted Muhammad ﷺ to be part of their group in order to prevent the Jews from claiming him as their own.[1]

During the following pilgrimage season approximately twelve people from the tribe of Khazraj took the oath of allegiance to Islam. In the next year (the twelfth year of the mission), a much larger number of about seventy-two accepted Islam. The oath, called "The Pledge at al-'Aqabah"[2], which Muhammad ﷺ took with the Madinans said, in part, "Not to associate anything with God ﷺ (*shirk*); not to steal, fornicate, slander anyone, kill any offspring and not to disobey what was right." Muhammad ﷺ promised solidarity with the Madinans saying, "Your blood is my blood. Your destruction is my destruction. You are of me, and I am of you. I shall fight whomsoever you fight and make peace with whomsoever you will make peace."

The Prophet ﷺ sent back to Madinah with them an instructor Mus'ab bin 'Umayr. Remembered as "The Reader", he was responsible for teaching them Islam and the Qur'an. The precedent for carefully selecting individuals to teach and lead was set.

Muhammad ﷺ accepted the Madinan invitation to migrate to their city. As always, he was thorough and meticulous in his preparation. The first Muslims who were told to migrate were the most vulnerable, the women and the slaves.

It was now the thirteenth year of the Messengerhood. Except for Muhammad ﷺ, Ali, Abu Bakr and a few other Muslims, everyone else had left Makkah. The Quraysh had finally realized what was happening. They were chagrined at having overlooked the clandestine migration of Muslims to Madinah and now felt threatened by the opening of a new avenue for the spread of Islam. Their chance to snuff out Islam was inexorably slipping away. They came up with a bold solution that would root out the problem once and for all: to assassinate the Prophet ﷺ. To immunize themselves against retaliation, members of each tribe would participate, thus distributing the responsibility and the blame.

The Migration (Hijrah)

Muhammad ﷺ became aware of the plan to assassinate him and started to plan for the migration discreetly. Abu Bakr was asked to prepare two camels for the journey. Ali was asked to sleep as a decoy in the Prophet's ﷺ bed the night of the migration. The assassins who were spying on Muhammad ﷺ were fooled. This allowed time for Muhammad ﷺ and Abu Bakr to escape and hide in a cave in Mount Sur, about three miles to the east of Makkah and a mile above sea level, until the pursuit had died down.

Chapter IV: Unexpected Avenue for Expansion: Hijrah

If ye help not your leader (Muhammad), (it is no matter):
<u>For Allah did indeed help him,</u>
<u>when the unbelievers drove him out:</u>
He had no more than one companion (Abu Bakr):
They two were in the cave, and he said to his companion
"Have no fear, for Allah is with us"
Then Allah sent down His peace upon him...
(Qur'an 9:40)

The arrival at Madinah could not have been more different than the departure from Makkah. The entire populace seemed to be out in the streets. The city was buzzing with expectation and joy, little girls were singing his praises, and families were competing with each other to host him. To avoid showing any kind of favoritism, Muhammad ﷺ chose to stay as a guest with Amr bin Awj , in front of whose house his camel had spontaneously halted. The tradition of weekly congregational prayers was started on the first Friday of his arrival in Madinah.

O ye who believe! When the call is proclaimed to prayer
on Friday (the day of assembly) hasten earnestly to the
remembrance of Allah.
(Qur'an 63:9)

Just before the migration, another important event had taken place. The danger to Muslims in Makkah was in extremis and there was a realistic possibility of their total eradication. Muhammad ﷺ received divine permission, through the instrument of *Wahy,* to fight back in self-defense against those who violently oppressed the Muslims.

<u>Permission is given (to fight) those who have taken up</u>
<u>arms against you wrongfully</u>.
And verily Allah is well able to give you succor.
To those who have been driven forth from their homes for
no reason than this that say "Our Lord is Allah."
<u>Hath not Allah repelled some men by others,</u>
<u>cloisters and churches and synagogues and mosques,</u>
<u>wherein the name of Allah is ever mentioned,</u>

> *would assuredly have been pulled down.*
> *Verily, him who helpeth Allah, Allah surely helps.*
> *For Allah is indeed Right, Powerful, and Mighty.*
> *Those who, if we establish them in the land, will observe prayer and pay the poor due and enjoin in what is right and forbid what is wrong,*
> *The final issue of all things rests with Allah.*
> *And if they charge thee with imposture, then (bear in mind) that already before them (there have been other people who had behaved likewise with their prophets such as) the people of Noah, and 'Ad and Thamud...*
> *(Qur'an 22: 39-42)*

> *Fight in the cause of Allah those who fight you,*
> *But don't transgress limits;*
> *For Allah loveth not the transgressor.*
> *And slay them wherever you catch them,*
> *And turn them out from where they have turned you out;*
> *For tumult and oppression are worse than slaughter;*
> *But fight them not at the sacred Mosque,*
> *Unless they first fight you there;*
> *But if they fight you, slay them;*
> *Such is the reward of those who suppress faith.*
> *But if they cease,*
> *Allah is oft forgiving, most merciful.*
> *And fight them on until there is no more oppression,*
> *And there prevail justice and faith in Allah;*
> *But if they cease let there be no hostility except to those who practice oppression*
> *(Qur'an 2: 190-193)*

Migration (*Hijrah*) to Madinah is a watershed in Muhammad's ﷺ mission. One of the first public acts as he took charge of the city of Madinah was to build a mosque (*Masjid*) historically known as the *Masjid an-Nabawi* or the Prophet's Mosque. Next he set about getting all parties together to sign a covenant, arguably the first of its kind in history, which would set standards for pluralism, tolerance and cooperation between various religious and ethnic communities.

Chapter IV: Unexpected Avenue for Expansion: Hijrah

The Covenant of Madinah ("...Conditions must be fair and equitable to all.")

The agreement that Muhammad ﷺ successfully persuaded the two Arab tribes of Aws and Khazraj, as well as the three Jewish tribes residing in Madinah to sign is called the "<u>Covenant of Madinah</u>". This covenant set out many of the principles essential to the peaceful functioning of a pluralistic society. It gave equality to all its citizens and accepted the coexistence of different religions in the community. All religious, ethnic and tribal groups had equal protection, rights and dignity. Muhammad's ﷺ inspiration for this pluralistic model was the Qur'an, which makes it incumbent upon Muslims to accept and respect all the previous messengers without distinction and respect their communities.

> *Say, "We believe in Allah*
> *and that which has been sent down to us*
> *And that which was send down to Ibrahim (Abraham),*
> *Isma'il (Ishmael), Ishaq (Isaac),*
> *Ya'qub (Jacob) and his progeny,*
> *And that which was given to the Prophets from their Lord*
> <u>*And we make no distinction between any of them*</u>
> *And to Him we are resigned*
> *(Qur'an 2:136)*

The concept of the "Ummah", the community of the believers and their allies, supporters and friends, was advanced for the first time in this covenant and laws respecting life and property were enunciated. Madinah was to be a sanctuary for all signatories of the covenant. Treachery was discouraged and loyalty encouraged. The phrase "loyalty is a protection against treachery" appears many times in the text of the covenant. The full text of the covenant is in the appendix.

Pluralism - The Islamic view

The concepts laid out in the "covenant" provide an outline for a pluralistic society. Pluralism is essential in ensuring dignity to minorities in any multi-religious society. Even in countries where, for all practical purposes, there is only one religion, there are sects and groups within the religion that demand the protection and spiritual and intellectual freedom which pluralism offers. The concept of pluralism differs substantially from tolerance alone. Pluralism presupposes equality amongst various groups, rather than one elite group merely tolerating another inferior group out of charity. It allows for coexistence of different religious communities that live by their own beliefs, judge themselves by their own laws, and help each other against any outside threat.

The Qur'an may be the only major scripture which talks explicitly about pluralism.

Verily they who believe (in the message of Qur'an)
And they who are Jews, Christians, and Sabeans (a
religious group whose identity is obscured by history)
<u>*Whoever believes in Allah and the Last Day,*</u>
<u>*and does that which is right*</u>
<u>*Shall have their reward with their Lord.*</u>
Fear shall not come upon them
and neither shall they grieve.
(Qur'an 2:62)

The Qur'an also condemns the antithesis of pluralism that is "Particularism" (a theological belief that only an elect few who follow a particular faith are eligible for redemption).

And (both) the Jews and the Christians say, "We are
Allah's children, and His beloved ones"
Say! Why then does He cause you to suffer for your sins?
Nay you are but human beings of His creating
<u>*He forgives whom He wills*</u>
(Qur'an 5:18-19)

Emphasis upon community (Ummah) in Islam

Islam places as much emphasis on the establishment of a just and social community as it does on attaining personal piety. Hypocrisy is defined as public display of piety and private acts of uncharitable behavior.

> *Seest thou one that denies the Faith*
> *Such is the man who repulses the orphan*
> *And discourages the feeding of the indigent*
> *So woe to those who offer the prescribed prayer*
> *But are unmindful of the purpose (underlying it)*
> <u>*Who only make a show of devotion*</u>
> <u>*But refrain from even elementary acts of kindness*</u>
> *(Qur'an 107: 1-7)*

Symbolic of the importance of society over the individual is the fact that worship in a group is deemed more desirable than in solitude. It was therefore quite natural that the Masjid became the center of all activities in Madinah. It was the focal point around which all activities of the community, religious, social, political and economic were conducted.

The Prophet ﷺ didn't have a house separate from the Masjid and small rooms were built along the perimeter of the Masjid for his wives. In one corner of the Masjid was a flat platform (*as-suffah*), where visitors who had no other place to stay would sleep. Prominent among the "people of *as-suffah*", a few years later, was Abu Hurayrah, the famous chronicler of the Prophetic traditions. The first few days in Madinah also saw the beginning of the "*Adhan*" or the call for prayer.

Another notable act in building a cohesive Ummah was that the Madinans, called the *"Ansars"* or helpers, who took on all of the responsibilities of the Migrants or *"Muhajirun"* (approximately forty five in number at that time), and treated them as their brothers.

> *Verily, they who have believed and left their homes and*
> *staked their lives and wealth in the cause of Allah,*
> *And also they, who have given shelter and help to them,*
> *These shall be friends the one to the other...*
>
> *They who have believed and left their county and*
> *struggled in the way of Allah,*
> *And they who have given the Prophet*
> *and his followers asylum,*

*And been helpful to them, these are verily the faithful.
Mercy is their due and an honorable provision.
(Qur'an 8:72 and 74)*

In a very short period after the Migration to Madinah, Muhammad ﷺ had proven himself capable of uniting various factions and setting exemplary standards of cooperation between them. He made a seamless switch from being a person under constant persecution to a leader with a large administrative and judicial responsibility. However this phase provided only a short respite before the next period of his mission, which was marked by crucial battles for survival of the Muslim community.

---

[1] Guillame, ***The Life***, p 197.

[2] *Ibid*, pp. 198-204.

Chapter V

A Clear Change in Direction and the Battles for Survival

*And from wheresoever thou issueth forth,
turn thy face toward the Holy Mosque
(Qur'an 2:150)*

Chapter V: A Clear Change in Direction and the Battle for Survival

The Courageous Yet Reluctant Warrior

The next phase in the Prophet Muhammad's ﷺ mission started out with a change in the *Qiblah* (direction for prayer) with a concomitant change in the nature of his struggle. His small community spent the next few years defending itself militarily in several battles that were imposed upon it by the Quraysh. The three major battles: Badr, Uhud, and Ahzab (Khandaq), which were critical in the survival of the life of the Muslim community, were fought over the next four years.

Change In the Direction Of Prayer (Qiblah)

While in Makkah, the Prophet ﷺ would frequently pray standing at the same place where Ibrahim ؑ had prayed. This allowed the Muslims to pray simultaneously in the direction of the Ka'bah and Jerusalem. The Makkan Arabs, on the other hand, prayed only in the direction of the Ka'bah and the "people of the book" in the direction exclusively of Jerusalem. After he arrived at Madinah, Muhammad ﷺ initially prayed in the direction of Jerusalem. However, in the second year after the migration (*Hijrah*)he received a revelation, in the middle of a prayer, to change his direction toward the Ka'bah.

And from wheresoever thou issueth forth,
<u>turn thy faces (for prayer) towards</u>
<u>the holy mosque al- Masjid al-Haram</u>
And wherever ye are, then turn your faces towards it,
So that men might have no grounds to dispute with you
except those of them who are deviators.
(Qur'an 2: 150)

The somewhat cryptic explanation given in these verses for the change in direction of prayer (*Qiblah*) appears to indicate that the reason for the switch was to clear up any misunderstanding people might have had about the separate identity of this emerging religion, whose name Islam had not been revealed yet. In another verse, the Qur'an appears to downplay the importance of the change in *Qiblah* in this fashion.

> *Now the erratic among the people will say:*
> *"What hath turned them (the Muslims) away from the*
> *Qiblah to which they used to turn hitherto!"*
> *Say, "The East and the West are Allah's,*
> *He guideth whom He will to the straight path."*
> *(Qur'an 2:142)*

Nevertheless one practical result of the change in Qiblah must have been that some of the Jews who hypocritically prayed with the Muslims when the direction was Jerusalem, but now found it very difficult to do. Muhammad ﷺ was clearly distancing himself both from the Jews and the non-Muslim Arabs.

As symbolized by the change in direction of the prayer, the new assertiveness of the community was also seen in their beginning to defend themselves rather than remain passive recipients of abuse. As mentioned earlier, this necessity to defend themselves was essential for the survival of the community. The increasing influence of Muslims in Madinah and their increasing self-confidence further reinforced Qurayshi militants urgent desire to destroy the Muslims.

The Quraysh would not leave the Muslims alone in Madinah. Abdullah bin Ubayy, a prominent leader and potential rival of Muhammad ﷺ in Madinah, received from the Quraysh a letter which warned him to, "... kill Muhammad, or expel him from Madinah, or else risk destruction..."[1] This threat was perceived to be so real that the Muslims would stay awake all night in turns to watch for any surprise attack. It was also decided to set up a mobile defense force for constant surveillance and interdiction of any attacking forces.

The Muslims sent out expeditions to form pacts with the neighboring tribes who were prevented from visiting with Muhammad ﷺ. Expeditions were also sent out to disrupt Qurayshi trade caravans, but there was to be no bloodshed. During one of these trips, when a Muslim killed one of the Qurayshi caravan members, he was severely reprimanded. The prominent Muslim historian at-Tabari records Muhammad ﷺ

as saying, "You did something (looting the caravan) which you did not have permission to do. You fought in the sacred month, when you had orders not to do so."[2] The Muslim responsible for the transgression was asked to pay "just recompense"[3] to the family of the man killed. This incident, according to at-Tabari, was the event that galvanized the Quraysh to attack the Muslims, resulting in the battle at Badr.

The Battle of Badr

The battle of Badr may have been no more than a skirmish by the standards of war such as humankind has engaged in. However in its symbolism and potential significance for the survival of Islam, it was clearly one of the most important in Muslim history. This battle, the first ever fought by Muslims, took place two years after the migration to Madinah, (which was the fifteenth year of Muhammad's ﷺ twenty-three year mission), at an oasis located approximately eighty miles southwest of Madinah.

Muslims in Madinah received intelligence reports that the Quraysh were preparing to launch a major assault on them with the intent of wiping them out permanently. Another scout reported that a trade caravan led by a Qurayshi opponent of the Muslims was in the vicinity. It was unclear whether the Muslims would meet this caravan or the Qurayshi army if they ventured out. Muhammad ﷺ gathered his followers together and asked them if they were willing to fight with him. Miqdad b. 'Amr, one of his companions, gave a memorable reply, "We are not like Musa's (Moses) people to say, why don't you and your Allah fight. We will be to your right and to your left, behind you and in front of you."[4] There were a total of 313[5] (sixty Muhajirs, and 253 Ansars) men with the Muslim army.

The Quraysh had been preparing for a confrontation with Muslims for a long time. They felt that this was the opportune time to destroy the Muslims, and they set out to do so with a well equipped force of a thousand men, hundreds of them on horses. The two forces camped out at Badr. When they met the battle surprisingly resulted in an overwhelming victory for the much smaller and poorly equipped Muslim force over the Quraysh. In retrospect, it is easy to see why Muslims won so decisively. The Muslims were clearly highly motivated and well disciplined. The Quraysh, in contrast, were divided amongst themselves and their motivation was entirely negative, that is for revenge. Even the weather seemed to favor the Muslims. The rains that fell the previous day had turned their side of the battlefield into a muddy ground with a poor foothold. The assault on the Quraysh was so fierce that they imagined many more Muslims than were actually engaged in battle. Verses from *Surat Anfal* provide remarkable insight into the battle of Badr.

> *Remember how thy Lord caused thee (at Badr)*
> *to go forth from thy home in the cause of truth,*
> *And how some of the believers were quite averse*
> *to go forth (with thee).*
> *(On that occasion) they disputed with thee over the rightness, (of the steps to be taken) which had been made so clear to them;* <u>*They thought they were being led forth to death with eyes wide open.*</u>
> *And (O ye believers! remember) when Allah promised you that one of the two (enemy) parties should fall into your hands (trade caravan or the Qurayshi forces),*
> *While you desired that they who had no arms should fall into your hands, On the other hand Allah proposed to prove the truth of His words by rooting out the unbelievers, (who were fully armed).*
> *That He might prove that truth always prevails and falsehood comes to naught,*
> *However much the evil- minded may dislike it.*
> *(Qur'an 8:5-7)*

The Qur'an alludes to the Muslim motivation during the battle.

> *On that occasion (O Prophet!) thy Lord inspired the angels with the assurance,*
> *"I will be with you, therefore, steady the hearts of the faithful, I will cast dread*
> *into the hearts of the unbelievers."*
> *(Qur'an: 8- 12)*

Chapter V: A Clear Change in Direction and the Battle for Survival

On that day when you were camped on the near side of the valley and the enemy on the further side, and the caravan was further down your encampment.
Had you ever agreed (among yourselves) to decide upon an engagement with the enemy, you would have failed to proceed with your decision
(for fear of not being a stronger force).
But Allah led you into action notwithstanding that He might accomplish the thing decreed by Him to be done. (Such was the decree of Allah that it had become so manifest to everyone at the moment).
<u>*That they who were perishing realized*</u>
<u>*that Allah was not on their side.*</u>
<u>*And they who were winning that Allah was on their side.*</u>
Verily Allah is Hearing, Knowing!
(Qur'an 8:42)

And finally

<u>*(O believers) you have no other alternative except to fight them till persecution ceases,*</u>
And the true way of life is pursued
in absolute devotion to Allah.
But if they give up (fighting), Allah will take note of what they do thereafter, But if they do not respond (to this call for peace, then do not lose heart),
rest assured that Allah will protect you.
Excellent protector indeed is He and excellent Helper.
(Qur'an 8:39)

Although now the victory at Badr appears predestined, at the time the battle occurred, it was uncertain whether any Muslims would survive. Nothing in the life of the nascent community had been so perilous nor carried the potential of such complete defeat.

Humane treatment of prisoners of war (POWs)

The battle of Badr saw the first capture of POWs by Muslims. The directive from the Prophet ﷺ was to treat them as if they were family members. The result was that the captives were often fed better than the captors themselves. Some of the captives were so surprised and impressed by the behavior of their captors that they accepted Islam. As there was no Qur'anic directive on how to deal with them, various options were discussed. The Prophet ﷺ favored those who advised freedom after restitution. Those who could not pay monetary restitution were asked to teach ten individuals to read and write. According to Cherif Bassiouni of DePaul University (Chicago, IL), this is the first time in recorded history that POWs were treated humanely as a policy.

During the second year of *Hijrah*, *Sawm* (Fasting) in the month of Ramadan was made compulsory and the first congregational prayer of *'Id al-Fitr*, feast of breaking the Fast, was held in this year.

The Battle of Uhud

The time that elapsed between the battle of Badr and the next phase, which began with the peace treaty at Hudaybiyah, was perhaps the most physically dangerous phase of the Prophet's ﷺ mission. The humiliating defeat at Badr could not go unanswered by the Quraysh. They returned the following year (the third year of Migration or the sixteenth year of the mission) better prepared and motivated by a desire to avenge their defeat at Badr. Just as he had at Badr, Muhammad ﷺ consulted with his companions about the best strategy to follow. As suggested in the Qur'an, he was setting an example of conducting community affairs by mutual consultation (*Shura*). It is worth noting that the Qur'an includes mutual consultation in its definition of righteousness.

Those who hearken to their Rabb (Sustainer)
And establish prayers
And conduct their affairs by mutual consultation (Shura')
And spend on others (needy)
out of what was bestowed on them for sustenance
(Qur'an 42:38)

He accepted the majority preference to go out of Madinah

and meet the Qurayshi armies at the outskirts at a place called Uhud, rather remaining inside the fortifications to fight. The battle turned into an almost complete and disastrous rout. Approximately seventy of the 700 Muslims were killed and Muhammad ﷺ, who was then 56 years old, suffered a blow to his face which knocked out some of his teeth. In stark contrast to the Muslims' humane behavior towards the defeated Quraysh in Badr, the Quraysh tortured Muslims who were captured following this war.[6] The bodies of some of the dead were mutilated. The most gruesome of these mutilations was that of Hamzah's (the Prophet's ﷺ uncle and staunch supporter) body by a woman named Hind, the wife of Abu Sufyan, a Makkan aristocrat.

The Qur'an speaks about Uhud in the following Verses:

Allah indeed did keep His promise to you so long as you were engaged in (war) accordance with His directions.
And had not flinched and begun to dispute among yourselves about the order (that a party should stick to a particular post till the end).
And disregarded instructions the moment when (the prospect of victory was in sight and) you saw the (booty) for which you had a liking.

(The main reason for the loss was that a group of Muslims who were designated to guard the rear, left their position to join others in collecting war booty. This act of greed allowed the enemy to regroup and attack from the rear.)

For among you were some who desired this world and some who desired the next.
Then in order to make trial of you; He diverted your attention from them (your foes).
Yet, He hath forgiven you,
for Allah is indulgent to the believers.
Remember the occasion when the Prophet was from the rear calling you and you were rushing up the heights (of the mountain) taking no heed of anyone!

(As his companions fled up the mountain Muhammad ﷺ

stood his ground rallied his forces.)

Then you had to go through trial after trial that you might not hereafter rue the loss of anything or bemoan over anything that might befall you.
Allah is aware of what you do.
Then after the tribulation, (Allah) caused calmness to descend upon you, and the sense of security seized a section of you, while another section obsessed in sheer ignorance, indulged in untenable suspicions against Allah.
They now say, "Did we have any voice in this affair?"
Say, "Verily, every affair rests with Allah."
In fact, they declare not to thee what they have hidden in their hearts.
They only say, "Had we any voice in this affair, none of us would have been slain here."
Say, "Even were you in your homes, those who were destined to be slain would surely have gone forth to the places where they had to die.
And (all of this has happened) that Allah might make manifest what was in your breasts and purify your hearts."
And Allah knoweth what your hearts harbor.
(Qur'an 3: 152-154)

The various tribes around Madinah, who had been awed by the Muslim victory at Badr, became difficult and challenged the Muslims after the near defeat at Uhud. A few Muslims were killed in several minor skirmishes. During one of the skirmishes a companion of the Prophet ﷺ, Khubayb b.'Adi, was kidnapped and later executed by the Quraysh as an act of revenge.[7] His last request was to be allowed to pray before he was killed. After finishing a rather short prayer, he rose and said, "I wanted to pray longer, but (I was afraid) you may have misconstrued that I was afraid of dying!" An incredible act of courage in the face of death!

The Battle of Khandaq (The Trench)

The third major confrontation between Muslims and the

Chapter V: A Clear Change in Direction and the Battle for Survival

Quraysh occurred in the fifth year after the Migration. This was the last and the best organized attempt by the Quraysh to annihilate the Muslims. The Quraysh accumulated a major force of ten thousand. Muhammad ﷺ consulted with his close companions and took the advice of Salman al-Farisi (the Persian) to remain in Madinah and defend themselves by digging a trench along the side of the city which was most vulnerable to attack. Salman was familiar with the trench as a defensive strategy. Trenches were widely used in Persia, where he was born, but were a novel idea in Arabia. Again, Muhammad ﷺ was demonstrating the practice of mutual consultation, *wa amruhum shura Baynahum,* (and who conduct their affairs by mutual cosultation)[8] and innovation. The Jewish tribe of the Banu Qurayzah posed an additional potential risk to the Muslims in Madinah. The fortress in which the Qurayzah lived was behind Muslim lines. If the Banu Qurayzah reneged on their covenant with the Muslims to fight in concert against invading forces, and instead joined hands with the enemy, the Muslims would be caught between two hostile groups, greatly increasing risk of defeat. Once the Qurayshi armies arrived at the gates of Madinah, the Qurayzah did exactly that. They reneged on their covenant with the Muslims to defend jointly against invading enemies. The Muslims had a formidable force of Quraysh in front of them and the treacherous Banu Qurayzah behind them. The Qur'an records this event in the following words:

O ye who believe! Remember the favors of Allah had shown to you when the armies (of the enemy) came against you, and we sent a blast against them,

(This appears to be a reference to a cold front which came through one night and devastated the morale of the Qurayshi forces which were not prepared for it)

and also hosts which ye could not see. And Allah is watchful of your doings.

That was the occasion when the enemy forces had assailed you from every side, and that your eyes became distracted and your hearts seemed to come up to your throats, and you fell into diverse misgivings about Allah:

And at this moment a party of them (Munafiqs or hypocrites) said, "O people of Yathrib (Madinah)! You have no place of safety here, so turn back." Another party of them sought the Prophet's permission (to return) pleading, "Our houses are left defenseless." They were not defenseless, they only desired to flee.

Say to them (O Prophet!), "Flight shall not profit you, if ye try to flee away from your death or slaughter, you can only enjoy (security) but for a fleeting moment!"
(Qur'an 33:9-10,13 and 16)

The Khandaq episode turned into a victory for the Muslims without a battle actually being fought. The enemy forces were completely frustrated by the trench. They had never seen such a tactic used in a battle before and they were unable to cross it. They laid siege to the city for approximately a month, and after multiple attempts at crossing the trench, they and their allies ran out of patience and provisions, gave up and went home. The last straw was the cold wind in which they could keep no fires lit.

The Three Jewish Tribes of Madinah (Jealousy, Treachery, Tragedy)

The fate of the three Jewish tribes of Madinah is closely linked with the three major battles, which decided the fate of the Muslim community. The tragedy can be seen in what could have been rather than what actually transpired.

Muhammad ﷺ had clear expectations for the Jews and Christians of Arabia from the very beginning. He knew that the "people of the book", as the Qur'an calls them, were familiar with the concepts of monotheism and righteousness, that they had clear Messianic expectations. He expected them to recognize him as a Messenger of Allah ﷻ. The clarity, sanity, and truthfulness of the Qur'anic message, he thought, would turn them toward Islam. Some "people of the book" did accept

Chapter V: A Clear Change in Direction and the Battle for Survival

the message.

And when they (the Christians) hear what hath been sent down to the Apostle, thou wilt see their eyes overflow with tears because of the truth which they recognize.
They say, "Our Lord! We believe. Write us down therefore with those who bear witness."
(Qur'an 5: 83)

However most not only rejected the Qur'an's message but also showed hostility. This was especially true of the Jews of Madinah. They felt that any new Prophet ﷺ should come from amongst them, the "chosen people". Muhammad's leadership threatened their political power in Madinah, and so they regarded him as an enemy.

As mentioned earlier, one of Muhammad's ﷺ first acts on arrival at Madinah was to gather all the major tribes together, including the Jewish tribes to sign a Covenant. One of its major articles was the agreement to defend jointly against a common enemy. The tribe of Banu Qaynuqa' was the first to violate the treaty with the Muslims. The reason for this appears unclear, but it seems that the victory at Badr increased Muslim prestige, which they viewed as a direct threat to Jewish influence and prestige in Madinah. For the Qaynuqa', who had the reputation of being the most fearless and proud tribe in the area, the increase in Muslim prestige resulted in a clear diminution of their standing in the community. In a society that functioned on social pride this was a serious matter and they became increasingly disagreeable and hostile towards the Muslims. In this tense atmosphere, there were many incidents of provocation. A Muslim woman was molested, for example, and in the ensuing fight a Jew and a Muslim were killed. As several articles of the Covenant had been breached repeatedly by the tribe of Banu Qaynuqa' the Muslims decided to besiege their fortress. After about two weeks of siege, the Qaynuqa' capitulated and were exiled.

Petty jealousy and hostility also motivated the clash with the Jewish tribe of Banu Nadir. After the battle of Uhud the Muslim position appeared much weaker. The Jewish tribes had excused themselves from the battle of Uhud, on the grounds of Sabbath, and had once again violated the Covenant. The Quraysh who expected the Banu Qurayzah to come to their help, may have instigated this. Abdullah bin Ubayy, a local chieftain with ambitions of being the leader of Madinah, had clandestinely promised to help them, causing the Banu Qurayzah to be even more arrogant and intransigent in their behavior. Following the battle, they even attempted to assassinate Muhammad ﷺ. They were also besieged in their fortress and soon capitulated.

*He it is who caused the unbelievers among the People of
the Book to quit their homes,
to join those who had gone into exile earlier.
Ye (believers) never thought they would quit their homes,
And even they (the People of the Book) on their part
thought that their fortresses
would protect them against Allah.
But Allah's force (the believers) came upon them from
whence they scarcely expected it.
(Qur'an 59:2)*

The Banu Nadir was permitted to take as many of their belongings as they could on their beasts of burden. Some of them ripped out the doors and windows of their homes and loaded them onto their camels. Many of them destroyed what was left of their homes so that it might not be usable to the Muslims. The Qur'an draws attention to this irony

*And caused such upheaval in their hearts that they let
their houses be demolished by their own hands.
(Qur'an 59:2)*

Referring to the hypocrites who had promised to help the Banu Nadir but did not, the Qur'an elaborates as follows:

*If they are expelled, they (the hypocrites among them) will
not go forth with them,
And if they are attacked,
they (the hypocrites) will not help them;
And even if these (make a show) of helping them, they will*

Chapter V: A Clear Change in Direction and the Battle for Survival

*do so only to turn their backs
so they will in fact receive no help at all*

*They (the People of the Book) will not fight you in a body
except from fortified towns or from behind walls.
They are themselves opposed to each other, and thou (O
Prophet) thinkest they are united (among themselves).
But at heart, they are not united.
This is because they are not a sensible people.*

*They are just like those who had preceded them and tasted
the results of their doings; So there awaiteth therein a
grievous chastisement.
(Qur'an 59:12, 14 and 15)*

The most tragic encounter with the Jews in Madinah was with the third and the last remaining Jewish tribe, the Banu Qurayzah. The expulsion of the Banu Nadir initially had a sobering effect and the Qurayzah revalidated the covenant with the Muslims. However, soon they were conspiring with both the pagans of Makkah and the Jewish tribes that had been expelled. When the Qurayshi armies attacked in what was later called the "battle of the trench" (*Khandaq*), the Qurayzah connived with them. If the invading army had been successful in breaching the trench, the Qurayzah would have attacked the Muslims from behind, resulting in total annihilation of the Muslim community. This was clearly a serious act of treason.

The Muslims had been extremely patient with the Jews. Their retaliation was proportionate, limited and just. With each breach of the treaty the penalty was increased. Even though the other two tribes had been expelled, the Banu Qurayzah had been given the benefit of the doubt. Nevertheless they reneged on the treaty, again with potentially dangerous consequences to the Muslims. After the battle of the trench was won, the fortress in which the Banu Qurayzah lived was besieged and they surrendered after a short while. As was Muhammad's ﷺ custom, they were judged by the rules of their own scripture, the *Tawrah* (Torah) and traditions (Talmud), and were asked to select an individual (Sa'd bin

Mu'adh), from their allies, the tribe of Aws, who they could trust as their judge.

And He brought down out of their fortresses such of the People of the Book (the Jews) as had aided (the confederates) and cast despair into their hearts.
Of these, ye slew some and some ye made captives.
And as heritage He gave you their land and their dwellings and their wealth, And further a territory on which you had never set foot.
And Allah hath power over all things!
(Qur'an 33: 26 -27)

Qur'an's Emphasis on the Nuclear Family

The fifth year of Hijrah also saw Muhammad's ﷺ marriage to Zaynab. She had been married to Zayd ibn Harith, who had been Muhammad's ﷺ slave. After freeing him, Muhammad ﷺ fostered him in his household. Muhammad's ﷺ marriage to Zaynab, after her divorce from Zayd appears to have caused some controversy. The Qur'an alludes to this controversy in the following words.

And call to mind the occasion when thou said to him (Zayd) on whom Allah had conferred a favor (made him a believer) and on whom thou also had conferred a favor (by adopting him), "Keep thy wife to thyself and fear Allah,"

(However Zayd decided to divorce Zaynab and Muhammad ﷺ thinks of marrying her but hesitates for fear of being misunderstood.)

Allah intended to bring to light that thou hesitated to avoid criticism from men (around you).

('Aishah is reported to have said, "Had the Messenger of Allah been inclined to suppress any of what was revealed to him, he would surely have suppressed this verse.)[9]

Better it would have been for thee to fear

> *(the disapprobation of) Allah.*
> *And (thou knowest that) when Zayd had settled to divorce,*
> *We gave her to thee in marriage that it might not be*
> *regarded as sin in the eyes of the faithful, should they*
> *marry the wives of their fostered sons when they have been*
> *freed from all obligation.*
> *And the behest of Allah has to be carried on*
> *unhesitatingly.*
> *No blame attacheth the Prophet in any matter concerning*
> *which Allah hath given him permission.*
> *Such way is the way of Allah*
> *with the Prophets gone before:*
> *The behest of Allah is thorough in taking account.*
> *(Qur'an 33: 37, 38)*

Zaynab's marriage to Zayd appears to have occurred under some duress, or more accurately, moral pressure. Muhammad ﷺ was keen on making the point that former slaves had the same status as anyone else in the society; Zaynab belonged to his tribe, and Zayd was a freed slave.

Muhammad's ﷺ subsequent marriage to Zaynab seemed designed to strike down the practice of treating adopted children as biological progeny. The Qur'an links the practice of artificially designating individuals as blood relatives with another societal aberration of punishing wives by calling them mothers. (The practice was called *Zihar,* which literally means back or turning your back on some one or neglecting or abandoning.) This unjust and callous practice of disowning one's wife by likening her to one's mother, thus perverting a natural relationship, was banned.

> *Allah hath not provided anyone*
> *with two hearts within him.*
> <u>*Neither hath He let you disown your wives by simply*</u>
> <u>*addressing them as your mothers,*</u>
> <u>*Nor hath He let your adopted sons*</u>
> <u>*be addressed as your own sons.*</u>
> *Such forms of address proceed from your mouths;*
> *But Allah speaks the truth and points out the true relationship between one and (his) mother.*

Name them (adopted sons) after their father;
before Allah, this will be more proper.
But if ye know not who their fathers are, then let them be
addressed as your brethren in faith and your friends.
And no blame however, is attached to you for using such
forms of address unless you have made them
with the intent of your heart.
And remember, Allah is indulgent in such matters,
the Merciful.
(Qur'an 33: 4- 5)

And again,

Muhammad is not the (literal) father of any of you,
But he is the Apostle of Allah and the seal of the Prophets
(closing the time of Prophethood):
And Allah knoweth all things.
(Qur'an 33: 40)

The aim of both of these injunctions was to stress and formalize a nuclear family, man, wife and children as a unit. The integrity of the natural family was protected against the introduction of all fictitious relationships, including relationships that the Arabs created even among adults.

Muhammad ﷺ as a Military Leader

The Prophet ﷺ and his followers were faced with very aggressive proponents of disbelief. The Muslims with the Prophet never intiated or instigated any wars. Muhammad ﷺ and the Muslims engaged in these battles with great discipline, avoiding injury to the innocent and using only the minimum force needed. Striking a blow in anger, even in battle, was prohibited.

Muhammad ﷺ was physically present on the battlefield in all of these wars risking his life and limb. His presence at the battlefield was essential in keeping the morale of his people high. The near defeats at Uhud and Hunayn would have turned into complete disasters except for his presence. He inspired the Muslims to remain steadfast and patient during that long siege at the battle of the Trench.

He used innovative strategies in the battles, which included the use of the trench as a defense. During the digging of the trench he was an active participant. He consulted frequently (*Shura*) and followed the majority opinion (*Ijma'*), even when it sometimes went against his own judgment.[10]

In addition to setting new standards for the humane treatment of POWs, the Prophet also implemented Qur'anic rules for the conduct of war, minimizing collateral damage, including minimizing damage to trees! Women, children and non-combatants were not to be harmed. When the enemy stopped fighting, he was to be given immediate sanctuary.

Fight in the cause of God against those who fight you, but do not transgress limits. God does not love transgressors.
(Qur'an 2:190)

If they seek peace, then seek you peace.
And trust in God for He is the One that heareth and knoweth all things.
(Qur'an 8:61)

Thus he established the doctrines of protecting civilians, limiting collateral damage, granting amnesty to the enemy when he stopped fighting, and treating POWs humanely. Only in the 20th century would other nations consider agreeing to such principles in the Geneva convention.

The Seven Phases of Prophet Muhammad's Life

[1] ***Sunan Abu Dawud***. ch. 2, p. 67 (One of the books of the traditions of the Prophet ﷺ, available in Arabic with a translation in the Urdu language).

[2] at-Tabari. ***Tarikh ar-Rusul wal-Mulk***. p. 1275 (now available in English translation).

[3] Just recompense or *Qisas,* the money which the victim's relatives might opt to receive in lieu of executing the murderer.

[4] Guillame, ***The Life***, p. 293.

[5] The number 313 has become sacred in Muslim tradition, as has the number 786 that stands for the word *Bismillah* or "I begin in the name of Allah." One illustration is the use of the number 786 in e-mail addresses by many Muslims.

[6] Guillame, ***The Life***, p. 387.

[7] *ibid.* p. 428.

[8] Qur'an 42:38.

[9] Muhammad Asad. ***The Message of The Qur'an***. (Gibralter: Dar al-Andalus Ltd., 1980) p. 646. (Asad refers to this statement from 'Aishah, in footnote 45, which is recorded in both in Bukhari and Muslim's books of traditions.)

[10] It is therefore surprising that the concept of mutual consultation has not taken root in Muslim societies. The democratic systems seen in parts of the Muslim world in the twentieth century are laudable but essentially transplants from Western models and not always suited to the local societal needs and imperatives. Following and adapting Muhammad's ﷺ use of consultation may have resulted in a more equitable and just system of governance in Muslim societies. For a comprehensive and thought full discussion of the topic please see John L Esposito and John O Voll. ***Islam And Democracy.*** (New York: Oxford University Press, 1996).

Chapter VI

The Peace Dividend: Hudaybiyah

Verily, We have granted thee a manifest victory.
(Qur'an 48:1)

Chapter VI: The Peace Dividend: Hudaybiyah

The Statesman Par Excellence and Teacher

After four years marked by the three major conflicts, Muhammad's ﷺ mission took another unexpected and peaceful turn. It is remembered in biographical books as the Treaty of *Hudaybiyah* . The events that led to this treaty were anything but promising. It was now six years after the Muslim Migration to Madinah and the verses establishing the central role of the Ka'bah in Makkah had been revealed.

... Now shall we turn thee to a Qiblah that shall please thee
Turn then thy face in the direction of the sacred Mosque
(Qur'an 2: 144)

Many Muslims were nostalgic for the streets of Makkah and pined to return to it for a visit. They were the only group denied the privilege of pilgrimage by the Quraysh. The Qur'an alludes to this Qurayshi intransigence in these verses.

But what plea have they
that Allah should not punish them,
<u>*when they try to keep (men) from the Sacred mosque-*</u>
They are not fit as its guardians.
No men can be its guardians except the righteous.
But most of them do not understand.
Their prayer at the House (of Allah) is nothing but
whistling and clapping of hands (its only answer can be)
"Taste ye the Penalty because ye blasphemed."
(Qur'an 8: 34-35)

Muhammad ﷺ had a dream in which he saw himself performing the pilgrimage. He joyfully announced a date for departing on the lesser pilgrimage ('*Umrah*) and invited everyone, including the surrounding tribes, to join him. It appeared to many like a death wish, so very few of the tribes accepted his invitation to join in the pilgrimage. The Qur'an chides those who excused themselves from the pilgrimage.

The desert Arabs who lagged behind will say to thee:
"We were engaged in (looking after) our flocks and herds, and our families.
Do thou then ask forgiveness for us?"
They say with their tongues what is not in their hearts.
Say! "Who then has any power at all (to intervene) on your behalf with Allah.
If His will is to give you some loss, or to give you some profit, but Allah is well acquainted with all that ye do."
Nay, ye thought that the Apostle and the Believers would never return to their families.
This seemed pleasing in your hearts, and ye conceived an evil thought, for ye are a people lost (in wickedness).
(Qur'an 48: 11-12)

The general reaction of the people in Madinah was surprise. The Prophet ﷺ was relying on the Quraysh to adhere to the old Arab practice of not engaging in warfare during the four sacred months. Nevertheless the Prophet ﷺ and his close followers left for pilgrimage essentially unarmed, dressed in traditional pilgrimage garb, and with the sacrificial camels in tow. There would be no doubt in anyone's mind about the peaceful intent of this group of pilgrims.

The Quraysh in Makkah were also surprised and became suspicious of this move. They were certain subterfuge was involved. They quickly gathered a cavalry of 200 and set out to intercept the Muslims. This force was led by Khalid ibn al-Walid, the same military leader who later accepted Islam and became the famous Muslim general. When the Prophet ﷺ learned of this impending cavalry attack, he changed his route to avoid confrontation, camping at a place called Hudaybiyah

"Woe to the Quraysh," said the Prophet ﷺ in frustration. "Why should they object to letting me finish this affair (pilgrimage)..." However, he still hoped for a peaceful resolution. "If the Quraysh would ask us for a guarantee of Muslim intentions based upon our blood relationship to them," said Muhammad ﷺ, "we should be happy to give it to them."[1]

There were several days of reconnaissance, negotiations and patient waiting but nothing seemed to go right. Local inhabitants attacked the Muslim camp one night. Many amongst the Muslims wished to retaliate, but Muhammad counseled patience. One reason for avoiding conflict was the fear that some of the Makkans who had accepted Islam but had not declared themselves openly would be inadvertently hurt.

And He it is who held back their hands from you and your hands from them in the valley of Makkah, After He had given you victory over them, And Allah seeth what ye do.
It is they who have disbelieved who kept you away from the sacred mosque and prevented the offering from reaching its destination (or the place of sacrifice).
<u>*Had there not been such believing men and women (among the Makkans), not knowing who were believers you might have trampled them.*</u>
<u>*And thus committed an offense in ignorance,*</u> *(though) Allah admits to His mercy whom He will, the unbelievers would (have been punished).*
And (on the other hand), had the believers and the unbelievers been clearly separated, We would have surely hastened a grievous chastisement on the unbelievers.
(Qur'an 48:24,25)

During the negotiation process, Muslims sent Uthman ibn Affan to Makkah as an emissary. He did not return for a while, which raised fears among the Muslims that he may have been murdered. The Prophet ﷺ gathered his followers under a tree and asked them to renew their pledge to be faithful to Allah ﷻ, and remain steadfast under all circumstances.

<u>*Allah's good pleasure was on the believers when they swore fealty to thee under the tree.*</u>
He knows what was in their hearts and He sent down tranquillity to them.
And He rewarded them with a speedy victory.
And they who have pledged fealty to thee (O Muhammad) have in truth pledged fealty to Allah.
And the hand of Allah (so to speak) rests on their hands (to symbolize the sanctity of the pledge given).
So whosoever shall break his pledge shall break it to his own hurt, And whosoever is true to his pledges given to

Allah, to him will He assuredly grant a high reward.
(Qur'an 48: 18- 10)

This pledge of fealty is remembered as *Bay'at ar- Ridwan* (Fealty of Allah's Good Pleasure). The Muslims demonstrated *nonpareil* courage and moral strength on this occasion. These 1400 to 1500 men and women with Muhammad ﷺ in Hudaybiyah were unarmed and faced the possibility of a massacre at the hands of the Quraysh. Soon thereafter however Uthman returned safely and a treaty was negotiated with the Quraysh. The terms of the treaty with the Quraysh appeared to decidedly favor the Quraysh. Muhammad ﷺ offered to compromise on every issue, even the signing of his name on the treaty as Muhammad, son of Abdullah, rather than Muhammad, the Messenger of Allah.

The treaty of Hudaybiyah, as it is known, called for Muslims to return to Madinah without performing the rites of pilgrimage. They would be allowed to come back the next year to perform the pilgrimage. All hostilities would cease for a period of two to ten years. Either side could form alliances with any of the tribes in Arabia. (The full text of the treaty is in the appendix.)

Many among the Muslims were disappointed at the whole affair, which looked like a humiliating defeat. It must have perplexed them when Muhammad ﷺ received a revelation calling Hudaybiyah a "manifest victory." However events over the next few years proved how beneficial this seemingly one-sided treaty was to the Muslims. The Qur'anic description of this event as a manifest victory was proven correct.

<u>We granted thee (O Muhammad) a striking victory</u>.
That Allah might compensate thee for the earlier and the later lapses (in war strategy) and consummate His blessings on thee, and direct thee to a right course of action (to follow hereafter).
Allah hath indeed fulfilled for His Apostle (in every detail) his dream (wherein he had heard Allah saying to him) "Ye shall assuredly enter the sacred mosque if Allah wills, in full security, with your heads shaved and your hair properly trimmed, fearing nothing,

Chapter VI: The Peace Dividend: Hudaybiyah

*For He knoweth what ye know not.
And besides this, <u>He hath granted you an early victory</u>."
(Qur'an 48:2,27)*

The two to three years of peace allowed freedom of movement for people across Arabia. Many tribal representatives visited Madinah and heard the Islamic message. More important they saw the practical application of the Qur'anic message in the metamorphosis of entire communities. The Muslims were able to send proselytizers to all parts of Arabia. The net result was an exponential increase in the numbers of Muslims in the peninsula. Muslims soon had the numbers and the momentum.

*When the Help of Allah cometh and (as a result of it cometh) victory.
And thou (O Muhammad!) shouldst see men accepting the way of Allah in large numbers.
(Qur'an 110:1-2)*

Muhammad ﷺ as a Statesman

In the sixth and seventh years after the migration, the Prophet ﷺ sent letters to a number of neighboring monarchs and rulers inviting them to Islam. He told his companions "Allah has sent me as a mercy for all humankind (and not just for Muslims). Do not differ amongst yourself like 'Isa's (Jesus) disciples. Take this message of truth to everyone."[2] The rulers of Rome, Persia, Egypt, Ethiopia, Yemen, and Sudan all received Muslim emissaries.

The Caesar of Rome received the message with a sympathetic ear, but did not convert to Islam.[3] The king of Persia considered the message to be an insult and tore up the letter. The ruler of Ethiopia sent back a courteous note stating that he considered Muhammad ﷺ a true Prophet. The monarch of Egypt sent the envoy back with gifts including two slave girls. One of them, Maria (the Copt) embraced Islam and the Prophet ﷺ married her as a sign of respect to the Egyptian monarch. The Yemeni ruler wrote back saying that the message was wonderful but he would only accept Muhammad's ﷺ sovereignty if he had a share in Muhammad's ﷺ power. The most hostile response came from the king of Sudan, who asked his army to get ready to prepare for an invasion. The message Muhammad's ﷺ emissaries took with them was a non-confrontational attempt at gaining adherents by persuasion. He had a clear message and none of what he was proposing was for personal or national aggrandizement. He was clearly pursuing high universal ideals and not narrow personal, tribal or national interests. His attempts to change minds were not mere rhetoric, but based on his own personal example and the model society he had established in Arabia. This theme of bringing change by inviting people to ponder the truth runs through all of the actions in his life's undertaking.

> *There shall be no compulsion in religion.*
> *(Qur'an 2:256)*

This was merely one of many examples of statesmanship exhibited by the Prophet ﷺ.

A statesman may be defined as someone who has the wisdom and vision to inspire policies and actions with long-term goals in mind, someone with breadth of view and idealism, someone who has the capacity to compromise with dignity, allowing all parties in a dispute to feel that they are victorious, and someone who is not short sighted, partisan or opportunistic.

In addition to the manner in which he invited the neighboring monarchs to Islam, at least five other incidents illustrate his statesmanship. These are the rebuilding of the Ka'bah, the covenant of Madinah, the treaty of Hudaybiyah, the victory over Makkah and the quelling of unrest amongst the *Ansar* at his alleged favoritism toward the *Muhajirun*.

Historians record an early incident that illustrates Muhammad's ﷺ capacity to resolve potential conflict with all parties involved coming away satisfied. The Ka'bah had suffered damage over time and was being rebuilt. It was time for the Black Stone (*al- Hajar al- Aswad*) to be returned to its original position. Because of the importance attached to this stone, the representatives of all of the tribes present wanted the privilege to replacing the stone. Muhammad ﷺ happened upon this scene and was asked to mediate this potentially serious dispute. His solution was to place the stone on his cloak, and ask all of the of the tribe members to lift the cloak, thus sharing equally in the glory and privilege of replacing it. Another lesson from this incident, appears to be about sharing a burden as well as sharing the glory. Lifting the stone after placing it on the cloak allowed one equal share in the privilege and also made the burden lighter. This deft handling of the situation may provide an insight into Muhammad's ﷺ being chosen as a Messenger of Allah ﷻ.

The covenant of Madinah and the treaty of Hudaybiyah, both great examples of statesmanship, are discussed above. The humility, compassion and forgiveness he demonstrated at the victory of Makkah[4] is discussed later in this essay. There is another incident worth scrutinizing in some detail.

Following the Ta'if expedition, Muhammad ﷺ distributed the war booty, with a larger share going to some of the *Muhajirun.* This caused dismay among the *Ansars,* and talk of favoritism. The Prophet ﷺ resolved the tense situation by giving an emotional speech to the Ansar that is recorded in Bukhari. In part he said, "Would you not prefer that others may take cattle and material goods home with them and that you would take home the Prophet."[5]

As illustrated by these incidents from his life, the Prophet ﷺ proved an exemplary statesman. He mediated disputes, defused potentially explosive situations with ease, allowing the parties in the conflict to walk away as friends and allies. He set yet unheard of standards in pluralism and tolerance. He was unafraid to take risks and compromise for the sake of peace. His emissaries to other nations brought with them a message of cooperation and seeking common grounds. When he gave a pledge, he always kept it. If the other party broke it, he would not flinch from measures that were appropriate to maintain the sanctity of the pledge. He was humble in victory, compassionate, and forgiving to even his most intractable opponents.

Events Leading Up To the Conquest of Makkah

The seventh year of the Hijrah saw the neutralization of

the Jews at Khaybar. The Jewish tribes who had been expelled from Madinah had settled in Khaybar and were constantly instigating other tribes to fight against the Muslims. When the Muslims learned that the Jews were organizing an army to attack them, Muhammad ﷺ decided to besiege them in their fortress in Khaybar, and soon the Jews were defeated. The same year saw Muhammad return to Makkah to perform the lesser pilgrimage ('*Umrah*).

One of the causes of the treaty of Hudaybiyah was that the Quraysh and the Muslims would consider an attack on their allies as an attack on themselves and a breach of the treaty. The eighth year of the Hijrah saw precisely that type of a breach. The tribe of Banu Bakr, who was allied with the Quraysh, attacked the tribe of Khuza'h, who had been the first tribe to ally themselves with the Muslims. The Quraysh brazenly supported the Banu Bakr, and the tribe of Khuza'h was defeated. The Quraysh were informed that the treaty signed at Hudaybiyah would be invalidated by this action unless they paid the conventional just recompense (*Qisas*) for those members of the Khuza'h tribe who were killed in the war, and that they immediately cease supporting the Banu Bakr. The Quraysh ignored the demand for just recompense leaving the Muslims no other choice but retaliation to maintain the sanctity of the pledge. This incident led to the invasion and conquest of Makkah by the Muslims, which began the last and final phase of the Prophet's mission. The overwhelming forces the Muslims had gathered for the invasion proved so intimidating that the Quraysh surrendered without offering any resistance. This action resulted in the nearly bloodless conquest of Makkah.

Chapter VI: The Peace Dividend: Hudaybiyah

[1] Guillame, *The Life*, p. 500.

[2] Muhammad Shibli Nu'mani. *Sirat an-Nabi.* (Lahore: Islamic Press, 1975). p. 430. (Published in Urdu). Nu'mani refers both at-Tabari and Ibn Ishaq as having recorded this quote from the Prophet ﷺ.

[3] See appendix for full text of the letter sent to Heraclius. It is nearly identical to the letters sent to the other monarchs mentioned above.

[4] I have discussed this in greater detail later in the monograph.

[5] *Sahih al-Bukhari.* tr. Muhammad Muhsin Khan. (India: Kitab Bhavan, 1987). I have discussed this in greater detail later in the monograph.

Chapter VII

The Final Phase: Victory with Humility

Today I have perfected for you your religion, and have bestowed upon you My bounty in full measure and am pleased to assign for you Islam as your religion.
(Qur'an 5:3)

Chapter VII: The Final Phase

The Compassionate Ruler and Spiritual Leader

The Conquest of Makkah

The final phase of Muhammad's ﷺ mission started with the conquest of Makkah, and was marked both by a clear sense of fulfillment of the mission and a feeling that it was ending.

During the three short years following Hudaybiyah and preceding the conquest of Makkah, the number of Muslims grew enormously. Muhammad ﷺ received deputations from the various tribes in and around Arabia and sent out emissaries to neighboring tribes and kingdoms inviting them to study and ponder over the message of Islam. Soon most of the tribes in Arabia had become allies of the Muslims and the Quraysh increasingly were an irrelevant force.

After the nearly bloodless conquest of Makkah, Muhammad's ﷺ first act upon entering the city was the announcement of a general amnesty. Next, Muhammad ﷺ and his associates entered the Ka'bah and cleared out its many idols. As the idols toppled, he kept repeating the verses:

The truth has come and falsehood has passed away
Verily, falsehood is sure to pass away.
(Qur'an 17: 81)

The Messenger of Allah ﷺ then stood at the door of the Ka'bah and gave a brief speech. "There is no deity but Allah; He has no associate. He has made good and helped his servants. He alone has put the confederates to flight. I abolish every claim of privilege of blood or property, (i.e. the old practice of revenge), except the custody of the temple and providing drinking water to the pilgrims... O Quraysh! Allah has taken from you the haughtiness of paganism and its veneration of ancestors. Man springs from Adam, and Adam sprang from dust."[1]

He then read the following verses:

O mankind! Verily We have created you of a male and a female, and distributed you into tribes and families that ye might recognize one another.
Verily, the noblest of you, worthy of honor in the sight of Allah is he who is the most upright in character.
Verily Allah is knowing, the Cognizant.
(Qur'an 49:13)

He then asked the Quraysh, who were assembled in front of him, "What do you think that I am about to do with you?" When they expressed the hope that he would be good to them, he replied, "Go your way, for you are free." The themes he struck were of compassion, forgiveness, egalitarianism, brotherhood, and the abolition of the cruel pagan cycle of endless revenge.

The Near Defeat at Hunayn

Surprisingly, this magnificent conquest of Makkah did not end the wars for the Muslims. Soon after the triumph over the Quraysh at Makkah, the neighboring tribes of *Thaqif* and *Huwazin* decided to attack the Muslims. The conquest of Makkah had the paradoxical effect of making these tribes more hostile and aggressive than before. Muslims reluctantly went out to meet this assault.

(O believers!) This is a fact that Allah hath helped you on many a previous occasion.
And on the day of Hunayn, <u>when your numbers over which you had exulted availed you not,</u>
And the earth with all its vastness had straitened on you,
And you had to turn back in flight
<u>*It was then that Allah infused into the Prophet and those faithful (to him),*</u>
<u>*The spirit of steadiness and self-assurance*</u> *and succored them unseen hosts and defeated the unbelievers;*
and that is what the unbelievers deserved.
(Qur'an 9:25,26)

Chapter VII: The Final Phase

The above verses refer to the near defeat the Muslims suffered at Hunayn. Unlike the previous battles of Badr, Uhud and Khandaq, the Muslims were in larger numbers than the enemy but they seem to have been overconfident and poorly prepared. Al-Bukhari records that the Muslim army advanced initially, but many Muslims incorrectly assessed that the pagan tribes had been defeated and broke rank to collect the war booty. This act of indiscipline and greed allowed the pagans to regroup and attack. Finally, it was the courage and steadfastness under extreme danger of Muhammad ﷺ and a few of his companions, reminiscent of the battle of Uhud, which saved the day for the Muslims.

The defeated tribes retreated into the well-fortified city of Ta'if. Muhammad ﷺ and his army pursued them and laid siege to the town of Ta'if. Three weeks of multiple raids and bombardment of Ta'if proved fruitless. The Muslims decided to abandon the siege and return to Makkah. These pagans did not pose a significant threat, and Muhammad ﷺ had many other more important issues to pursue.

The Muslims had captured large amounts of booty, and large numbers of prisoners. When Muhammad ﷺ distributed the war booty, he appeared to give larger shares to those who had recently accepted Islam. This caused discontent and some unrest among those who had become Muslims earlier, especially the *Ansars* (Helpers). When Muhammad ﷺ became aware of this, he gathered everyone together and gave a memorable and emotional speech alluded to earlier in this essay. "Do you think ill of me in your hearts?" he asked. "Did I not come to you when you were errant and Allah guided you; you were poor and Allah made you rich, you were enemies (of truth) and Allah softened your hearts." He continued, "Are you disturbed because of the good things of this life by which I won over a people that they may become Muslims while I entrust you to your Islam? Are you not satisfied that (other) men should take away flocks and herds while you take back with you the Apostle of Allah? By Him in whose hand is the soul of Muhammad, but for those who migrated, I should be one of the *Ansar* myself. If all men went one way and the *Ansar* another, I should take the way of the *Ansar*."[2]

The Seven Phases of Prophet Muhammad's Life

Muhammad's ﷺ Disapproval of Superstitions

Ibrahim, Muhammad's ﷺ last son, died at one and a half years of age. This tragic event occurred on the day of a solar eclipse, which understandably seemed to justify an old Arab superstition about natural calamities and their effects on human affairs. Realizing this, Muhammad ﷺ made a remarkable pronouncement, rendering a fatal blow to the old superstitious practices of Arab society. "The sun and the moon," he said, "are signs of Allah's power. The birth or death of humans does not cause any eclipse."[3]

Gender Relationships

While the Prophet ﷺ was busy with major battles and affairs of state, there is evidence that jealousy and discord was brewing amongst his wives. Glimpses of this very private and human facet of his life are provided in the Qur'an.

And call to mind the occasion when the Prophet had given in confidence an information to one of his wives, and she had communicated it to another (wife).
And when Allah apprised him of this, he spoke of it to her in part and passed over the rest.
(Qur'an 66:1-5)

The verses quoted above allude to an incident in which two of the Messenger's ﷺ wives appear to have conspired with each other against a third wife. The two wives were gently admonished and all the wives were reminded that their status and duties, their rewards and punishments were higher than of any other women amongst Muslims. They were to be examples for the rest of the community. They kept their position by their own free will and could ask for divorce if they so desired. The Qur'an urges the Messenger's ﷺ wives to aspire for a higher calling and forgo the ultimately trivial material things in life.

O Prophet! Say to thy wives,
'If ye desire the life of this world

and its fineries (such as do not become
the wives of the Prophet),
Come, I shall offer you compensation and shall allow you
to leave me in a manner agreeable to you.
(Qur'an 33: 28)

Even these very private events in his life were public knowledge since they had implications and lessons for all. These events became occasions for revelation (*Asbab an-Nuzul*) of injunctions against backbiting and conspiring.

It is often unrecognized that gender relationships underwent quite a revolutionary change with the advent of Islam and the Messenger's ﷺ behavior. Spousal relationships were now based on love and compassion.[4] The Qur'an describes interdependency and love in marriage as follows

They are garments[5] (adornments) unto you as you are
garments (adornments) unto them
(Qur'an 2:187)

The relationships are to be full of love and tenderness.

And one of His signs is that He hath created for you
mates of your own species
that ye may find comfort in their company;
<u>And has put between you love and tenderness.</u>
Truly here are signs for those who reflect
(Qur'an 30:21)

There was levity and joy between spouses. "The best amongst you," he would often say, "are those who are best to your wives." On more than one occasion, much to the consternation, of his fathers-in-law, and companions Abu Bakr and 'Umar, the Messenger ﷺ could be heard having an argument with one of his wives. The established cultural tradition of women's inferiority and subservience to men was gone. The Prophet ﷺ sometimes helped out with household chores. Spouses in Islam were confidants, providers of solace and comfort, and advisors in crucial affairs. At Hudaybiyah he consulted with and took the advice of Umm Salamah, the wife who had accompanied him on the trip.

Mothers, both biological and foster-mothers, were shown great respect. Daughters were loved and were a source of joy and pride. The Prophet ﷺ would rise and kiss his daughter Fatimah, on the forehead, and his face wreathed in smiles whenever he met her. The false pride *(ird)*, which was partially responsible for female infanticide, disappeared from the society as in the blink of an eye.

Several injunctions about social behavior were promulgated, including modesty in clothing and contact with others.[6] The intent was to encourage interaction between men and women at an intellectual and spiritual level rather than a sensual level. Punishments for adultery and penalties for false accusation against others were formalized. A just and moral society built around personal piety based on the Qur'an was taking shape. The laws and edicts were rapidly changing both the private and public mores in a concrete and tangible form.

The Role and Status of Women in Early Islam

A review of women's status in Islam reveals the startling fact that the Qur'an recognized them as spiritual equals for the first time in world history. Moreover, for a long time Islam was the only religion that gave them such status with emphasis and clarity.

Indeed for all of them-the men who resign themselves to
Allah and the women who resign themselves,
And the believing men and the believing women,
And the devout men and the devout women,
And the truthful men and the truthful women,
And the men who are patient
and the women who are patient,
And the men who are endowed with humility
and the women who are endowed with humility,
And the men who give alms and the women who give alms,
And the men who observe the prescribed fast
and the women who observe the prescribed fast,
And the men who preserve their chastity

Chapter VII: The Final Phase

and the women who preserve their chastity,
And the men who oft remember Allah
and the women who oft remember Allah
For all of these Allah holds out forgiveness and great
recompense.
(Qur'an 33:35)

In this verse the Qur'an uses ten different adjectives to make its point that men and women are equal spiritually, with similar obligations and duties. There is no other verse where the Qur'an hammers home its intent with such emphasis. Moreover this is not the only verse, which deals with this issue.

The faithful, men and women, are friends one to the other;
They enjoin what is good and forbid what is evil;
They observe prayer and pay the poor-due and they obey
Allah and his Apostle (in every state).
Soon will Allah have mercy on them.
Verily Allah is the source of Power and Wisdom.
(Qur'an 9:71)

The Qur'an with unflinching regularity equates men and women spiritually. With equal unambiguity it recognizes differences in roles and responsibilities. Men are the protectors and solely responsible for the economic needs of the family. Women may earn and keep their income or spend it as they pleased.

The list of reforms Islam brought about is long. A brief catalog of these changes includes the following: female infanticide was banned; primogeniture was abolished; *Zihar* (the custom referred to earlier) was abrogated; incestuous relationships were made illegal and public indecency was wiped out. Women were given economic security and social privileges, such as to own and dispose of property, and the right to enter contracts and run businesses. Marriage became a contract between two consenting adults that was recorded in the presence of reliable witnesses. Divorce was discouraged, but in irreconcilable situations, it was allowed as a last resort. Women were given the right to initiate divorce proceedings (*khul'*) in case the husband was judged to be cruel or had deserted her. Polygamy was limited and was permitted mainly as a remedy for the vulnerable and exploited situation in which female slaves and orphans found themselves. Women and men were encouraged to become literate. Many women became recognized scholars in the Islamic disciplines.[7]

The intent of the Qur'an was to establish a just society by protecting its most vulnerable members, including the poor, the slaves, and those who were caught in the web of usury.

The Tabuk Expedition

In the ninth year of the *Hijrah,* Muhammad ﷺ received reliable information that the Roman army was gathering to attack the Muslims. The Roman emperor Heraclius began to see the Muslims as a threat. According to intelligence information, a well-equipped force of about forty thousand Romans were preparing to invade. The Muslims had no choice but to collect their own force and venture out to confront the enemy forces gathered at the border of Syria. As the Muslims prepared to venture out, they found themselves short of resources and manpower. When the call to arms went out, some came up with excuses, while others were upset that they lacked the means to join the Muslim army. The Qur'an recalls these events in the following verses:

(O Prophet!) Some of the Arab nomads came to you to offer excuses, praying for leave (to stay behind).
While others, having gone back upon their word given to Allah and His apostle sat at home.
So a grievous chastisement shall soon overtake these who have thus broken their pledge.
No blame shall lie on the feeble and the ailing and on those who have not the means to provide themselves (with war equipment if they should remain at home).
Provided that they are sincerely attached to Allah and His Apostle.
No blame shall lie on those who act righteously.
And Allah will cover their weakness and be merciful to them.
Nor shall blame lie on those who (having no conveyance

*of their own) came to thee that thou might
provide them with a mount;
Thou had to say, 'I can find nothing to mount on.' and they
had to turn away in anguish, their eyes shedding tears in
profusion for their inability to spend
anything in the way of Allah.
(Qur'an 9: 90-92)*

Muhammad ﷺ, as always, took the lead as the Muslims ventured out to meet the latest potential challenge. He assessed that the expedition was essential and so risks must be taken. The journey toward the enemy forces was long and arduous, with the outcome uncertain. As usual, the Prophet ﷺ demonstrated a great capacity to motivate, which explains why some of his companions wept because they couldn't accompany him on the expedition.

When the Muslim army reached the town of Tabuk, halfway between Makkah and Damascus, it turned out that the initial reports were only partially true. The Muslim army camped out at Tabuk for about twenty days and then returned to Madinah. In the Prophet's ﷺ absence, the group labeled the *Munafiqun* (the hypocrites) of Madinah had constructed a mosque, which had become a center of intrigue and controversy. When this became apparent Muhammad ﷺ ordered the mosque to be destroyed.

<u>*And there are some (from among the hypocrites) who have erected a mosque in sheer mischief and with a view to promoting unbelief.*</u>
*And causing a split among the believers and affording them a base for operation who had in the past warred against Allah and His Apostle.
They will surely swear,
"Our purpose was naught but good."
But Allah bears out that they are clear liars.
(O Prophet!) never step into it.
More worthy for you to enter is that mosque the foundation of which has been laid in piety from its very first day
(where you can lead the faithful in prayer) and to which repair those who aspire to unity;*

*And Allah indeed is pleased with those
who purify themselves.
Which of the two is better, he who hath laid the foundation
of his edifice on devotion to Allah and desires to please
Him, or he who hath raised it on the brink of a crumbling
bank which is bound to drag him into the fire of Hell?
Surely, Allah doth not guide those who commit excesses.
This building of theirs which they have built will not cease
to cause uneasiness in their hearts
until their hearts are torn to pieces.
And Allah sure is the Knowing, the Wise.
(Qur'an 9: 107-110)*

Rationale Behind Muhammad's ﷺ Battles

The expedition to meet the putative Roman attack was the last of the military engagements during Muhammad's ﷺ mission. It is worth reviewing this and other military engagements to understand the motivations behind them. It is a common criticism voiced by some writers that the Prophet ﷺ had changed form a exhorter to a conqueror, from a warner to a warrior, and in the interest of building an empire he had lost his spirituality. Nothing could be farther from the truth.

Muslims were permitted to fight, or more accurately fight back, to defend themselves, in the thirteenth year of Muhammad's ﷺ twenty-three year mission. At that point, the enemies of Islam were threatening to wipe out the Muslims. The permission to fight was limited and conditional.

*Fighting is now ordained for you, but this pleaseth you
not.
Perchance you dislike a thing though it is good for you;
And perchance you like a thing, which may be bad for you.
Allah knoweth.
But ye know not.
—And creating disorder (in the land) is more heinous than
manslaughter.
(Qur'an 216-217)*

Muslims could defend themselves, but they could not wage an aggressive war. When the enemy stopped, they had to stop as well.[8] The pagan practices of revenge killings, mutilation, torture, and disrespect of the dead were banned. Muslims who accidentally killed a non-combatant were reprimanded and asked to pay *Qisas* (just recompense). The rights of civilians and vulnerable members of the enemy were protected. Prisoners of war were to be treated with dignity and compassion. The Muslims were even prohibited from cutting down trees in enemy territory. The frequently heard adage "all is fair in love and war," clearly did not apply and was, in fact, considered a perverted practice.

Quraysh and other Arab tribes provoked four out of the five major battles, Badr, Uhud, Khandaq, and Hunayn. In many instances, fighting these battles appeared to be an open invitation for Muslims to commit self-annihilation. The courage displayed by the Muslims in these engagements equaled anything displayed at any time in human history. They fought for a cause they believed in, were unflinching in their steadfastness, and in every instance the Prophet ﷺ was among them fully exposing himself to the same risk he that asked his associates to face. The same qualities of extreme resolve and faith in their cause and leadership were displayed at Hudaybiyah.

The fifth war, the invasion of Makkah, followed the breaking of the Hudaybiyah covenant by the Quraysh. To return the Ka'bah to the fold of Islam was an extremely important objective in the minds of Muslims. The invasion of Makkah became inevitable after the brazen flouting of the treaty of Hudaybiyah by the Quraysh and their failure to agree to give restitution. As noted earlier, the conquest of Makkah was accomplished virtually without bloodshed. It set new and exemplary standards for conquerors. Muhammad ﷺ entered the conquered city of Makkah, on foot with his head bowed. There was no gloating, only humility and compassion. One of his first acts, after purging the Ka'bah of idols, was to issue a general amnesty. Even the most obnoxious enemies of Islam, who may have asked for clemency out of convenience rather than a change in heart and conviction, were forgiven.

Muhammad ﷺ was present with his companions at the

battlefield, in all five of the major battles. Many a time, his life was in danger and he was physically injured at least twice. His presence was a constant inspiration to his followers, and as a result in the battles of Uhud and Hunayn, near defeats were turned into victory. These battles were noble in their intent, necessitated by intractable circumstances, and set exemplary standards for compassion and respect for human rights.

So it was that we laid down for the Isra'ilites that if one slayeth another, for other than man-slaughter or for spreading disorder in the land, it shall be as if he has slain all mankind.
<u>*But if one saveth the life of a single person, it shall be as if he hath saved the life of all mankind.*</u>
Our Apostles have already come to them with clear proofs (of their mission and tried to dissuade them from their evil behavior), and yet many of them were there who nevertheless went on committing excesses in the land.
(Qur'an 5: 32)

The Pilgrimage (Hajj) by the Companions in the 9th Year of the Migration

In the ninth year of *Hijrah,* Muhammad ﷺ sent three hundred of his companions to perform the Hajj. This was the first pilgrimage performed with the fall of Ibrahamic rituals. Abu Bakr led the pilgrims; he explained the rituals of the Hajj and Ali read the first forty verses of *Surat at-Tawbah.*

(O ye believers!) Here is a declaration from Allah and His Prophet to those with who you have been in league till now, from among the (Arab) polytheists (that you are no longer in obligation to fulfill on your part the conditions of the covenant entered into with them)
Tell them, "You are now free to move about in the land as you like for four months." But bear in mind that you cannot weaken Allah on any account.
On the other hand, Allah will put to shame those who believe not in Him.

Chapter VII: The Final Phase

<u>*This is a proclamation on the part of Allah and His Apostle to those who assemble on the great occasion of the pilgrimage (Hajj) to the effect that Allah hath cleared Himself of all obligations to these polytheists even as does His Apostle.*</u>
So tell them, "If you turn to Allah even now, it will be better for you;
but if ye still decline to do so, make it clear to yourselves that ye shall not weaken Allah"
(O Prophet!) Announce to those who are not believers that a great chastisement awaiteth them.
(Qur'an 9: 1-3)

The Ka'bah was banned for the polytheists.

It is not for the polytheists to use for habitation the places reserved for the worship of Allah while they continue to be witnesses against themselves of infidelity to Allah.
These are the people whose works will come to naught and in Fire shall they abide.
He alone has the privilege to attend the places where Allah is worshipped who believes in Allah and the Last Day and observes prayer and pays the poor due and fears none but Allah.
These are they of whom it may be expected that they will prove themselves to be rightly guided.
...O ye believers! Surely those who prescribe partners to Allah are an unclean lot. Let them not after this approach the Holy Mosque, and if (due to lack of opportunity to profit by trading with them at the time of Hajj), you apprehend poverty, then (do not lose heart), Allah, if He please, will soon give you riches out of His abundance.
Verily, Allah knoweth (your needs), the Wise.
(Qur'an 9: 17-18 and 28)

The Struggle (Jihad) against Economic Oppression

The ninth year after the migration was also the year when directives about usury (*Riba*) were promulgated. The amount loaned to an individual would double (*Riba* means doubling) when the duration of the loan expired. This exploitative practice would make it impossible for the individual who had requested the loan to be ever able to return it. *Riba*, which was practiced widely, forced many people into economic slavery. Banning of *Riba* was an important part of Islam's fight against oppression. Other important facets of this effort against economic inequity and establishing social justice are compulsory sharing of wealth (*Zakah*), one of the five pillars of Islam, encouragement of voluntary giving (*Sadaqah*), strict injunctions against hoarding, and promotion of circulation of wealth in the community by investing in productive ventures.

The Concept of Jihad (The Noble Struggle)

Much has been written about the concept of Jihad and its misunderstanding by non-Muslims as "holy war." It would be useful at this point to discuss the controversy surrounding the use and misuse of this word. For Muslims, the concept is quite straightforward, and can be illustrated by the following anecdote. Once when Muslim soldiers were returning from a military engagement, their commander made the statement that "We are going from a lesser Jihad to a greater Jihad." The soldiers were surprised, and asked which military engagement they were headed for next. The commander replied that by "the greater Jihad" he meant *Jihad* or struggle against one's inner self (*Nafs*).

The word *Jihad* comes from the root letters *JHD,* which means to struggle or to strive. It is understood as a very positive, noble and laudatory term. That is how most piety minded Muslims understood the word and applied it in their personal, social, political and military lives. The history of the Muslims rulers, on the other hand, gives us examples of those who attempted to sanctify their wars of personal aggrandizement as wars for a noble cause by applying the label *Jihad* to them. A few even named their war departments as the departments of *Jihad.* This kind of behavior may be likened to the modern politician's attempt to wrap himself in the flag. It is easy to see through. Such exploitation of the term should not be allowed to corrupt the original or the commonly understood meaning of the word, which is to strive for the highest possible goals, struggle against injustice and practice self denial and self control to achieve the moral purity (*Taqwa*) to which all piety minded people aspire.

The "holy war" concept, for which many non-Muslims use the word *Jihad*, is foreign to Islam. Rather, it comes from a concept first used to justify the Crusades by the Christian Church during the Middle Ages. The concept of "holy war" also goes back to the time when the emperor Constantine the Great allegedly saw the vision in the sky with the inscription on the cross, "*in hoc signo vinces*" (in this sign you will be the victor).

The Arabic words for the term "the holy war" would be *al-harab al-muqaddash,* which neither appears in the Qur'an or the Hadith. None of Muhammad's ﷺ wars were fought with the objective and intent of converting people by force. In fact, as discussed earlier, these were defensive wars against groups who sought to eradicate Islam and the Muslims. In spite of that, the Prophet ﷺ always tried to avoid confrontation. Conversion was never sought by coercion, but by extending the invitation to study and ponder over the message of the Qur'an. He made an appeal to the intellect as well as the deepest instincts of mankind.

It is interesting and useful for social scientists or philologists to study how the meaning and usage of words differ in different communities. Ironically the word "crusade", because of its association with the crusades, should have a pejorative sense to it and yet the word has acquired an ennobled meaning in the West, even though the Church itself, along with most historians, acknowledge the injustice of the Crusades and the atrocities done in the name of faith. On the other hand, the word "*Jihad*" which means for Muslims, striving for the highest possible goal, for non-Muslims has acquired the negative and unjustified connotation of the holy war. Part of this modern legacy stems from the period of European imperial aggression, in which Muslims defended their homelands in a justified, defensive military response, invoking the term *Jihad* at times. Many European commentators at the time merely scoffed at their struggle, or met it with multiples of military force, invoking a "civilizing mission" to the benighted. In conclusion, it is important to be aware of how both words are used in the original context and meaning.

The Tenth Year of Migration (Hijrah)/The Farewell Pilgrimage

In the last year of his mission, the prophet Muhammad ﷺ decided to go on the Hajj pilgrimage. When this news became known, such large numbers of people came along that it looked as though the entire Arab nation was accompanying him. It was a climactic, majestic moment in the Prophet's ﷺ life. The success of the mission that once was in doubt had now been accomplished. As he spoke that day, sitting on his camel at the top of the hill in the plain of 'Arafat, he could see devout Muslims gathered around him all the way to the horizon. What once appeared impossible had come true in a most spectacular fashion. The time of troubles was behind him.

The Sermon at the Farewell Pilgrimage [9]

After completing the pilgrimage, the Prophet ﷺ stood on a small mountain (later called the mount of Mercy or *Jabl al-Rahma*) in the plain of 'Arafat and gave a sermon that had an air of finality to it. It was like the period at the end of a sentence, the last chapter of a book, the last act in a play. He spoke in the past tense. "Today, I have completed the *Din* (complete system of life) for you... and selected for you Islam."[10]

He began the speech by declaring, "All the pagan practices are crushed under my feet. O mankind, your Lord is One. Without doubt, your father Adam is one. No Arab has superiority over a non-Arab or a white over a black, or a black over a white, except on the basis of *Taqwa* (Allah consciousness). Each Muslim is the brother of another Muslim, and all Muslims are brothers. And as for your slaves, feed them what you eat, and clothe them with what you wear. All revenge from bloodshed during paganism is abolished. First and foremost, I forgive from my family, Rabi'ah bin al- Harith's son's murder. All usury is abolished. And first and foremost, from my family I abolish usury owed to my uncle, 'Abbas ibn 'Abdul Muttalib. Remember Allah in your dealings with women. You have rights over women, and they have rights over you. Your life and property are sacred to you till the Day of Reckoning."

After finishing the sermon, he asked, "When Allah will question you about me, what will you say?" The companions replied, "You delivered the message, you fulfilled your obligation." Muhammad ﷺ then raised his finger toward the sky and repeated three times, "*Allahumma Ashhad*" (O Allah, You are the witness). As he surveyed the crowd gathered to listen to him, he must have felt a sense of satisfaction. There are a number of other traditions attributed to this farewell pilgrimage. The four sacred months, in which all conflict was banned, were fixed. The practice of changing the months according to convenience was abolished.

The Final Illness

O men, If you have been worshipping Muhammad, then know that Muhammad is dead. But if you have been worshipping Allah, then know that Allah is living and never dies.
-Abu Bakr

The speech, which Muhammad ﷺ gave at the last pilgrimage and some of his other pronouncements, had the tone of a person who is bidding farewell. He appeared to have a premonition that his mission on this earth was coming to a close. His final illness lasted several days, producing a high fever and severe headaches. Occasionally, he fainted due to the extreme fever. Approximately four days before he died, he gave his last speech. He talked about the "choice" human beings have of striving primarily for success in this life or focusing on the hereafter. He stressed the Qur'anic concept that personal actions determine an individual's rewards. In a poignant Friday sermon he declared, "O Messenger of Allah's daughter, Fatimah, O Messenger of Allah's aunt, Safiyyah ibn 'Abdul Muttalib, perform righteous deeds for Allah, I cannot save you from Allah."[11]

After the sermon (*khutbah*) he went back to 'Aishah's chamber. The headache and the fever made him very uncomfortable. 'Aishah reports him as saying, "Jews and Christians have earned Allah's displeasure by turning the graves of their Messengers into temples of worship."[12] He was obviously thinking of his death and was worried that his followers might commit the same fatal error out of devotion and respect towards him. During the last day or two of his illness, he appeared to slip in and out of consciousness. He passed away in the month of May in the year 632 AD (the eleventh year of the Hijrah, in the Muslim month of *Rabi' al-Awwal*).

The news of Muhammad's ﷺ death spread rapidly. Most people were understandably in shock and disbelief. 'Umar was beside himself with grief, threatening to silence those who alleged the Apostle ﷺ had died. However Abu Bakr maintained his poise. When he returned to the Prophet's ﷺ house, he went up to the body, uncovered the Prophet's ﷺ face, and kissed him. Abu Bakr reportedly said, "... You (Muhammad) have tasted death Allah has decreed it. A second death shall never overtake you."

He then went out in the courtyard and spoke these memorable words. "O men, if anyone worships Muhammad, Muhammad is dead. If anyone worships Allah, Allah is alive, immortal."[13]

Then he recited the following verse:

Muhammad is no more than an Apostle.
Apostles before him have passed away.
If he dies or is slain, will ye then turn on your heels?
And he who turneth on his heels shall not in the least injure Allah.
And Allah will soon reward the grateful.
(Qur'an 3: 144)

Abu Bakr's actions and words at this emotional and critical moment in Muslim history had an impact on the course of Islam that is far more profound than most people realize. It prevented Muslims from succumbing to the very human instinct of deification of the Prophet ﷺ which people had done to the memory of many other messengers and charismatic leaders in the past.

Chapter VII: The Final Phase

[1] Guillame, ***The Life***, p. 552.

[2] *Ibid*, pp. 596-7.

[3] ***Sahih al-Bukhari***. vol. 2. Hadith 168. Narrated by al-Mughira ibn Shuba.

[4] Fazlur Rahman. "The Status of Women in Islam" ***Separate Worlds.*** (Columbia, MO: South Asia Books, 1971) pp. 285-311.

[5] The word garment is used to describe that which covers, protects and beautifies. The Qur'an uses the same term for piety (*Taqwa*).

[6] It is interesting to note that the *Hijab* as it is practiced today is not an early Islamic phenomenon nor is the practice of covering the face with a veil.

[7] The deviation from the Qur'anic norm, which is seen in many Muslim societies, is appalling and is a reflection of cultural practices supplanting the Islamic ideals.

[8] Qur'an 2:190-193.

[9] See appendix for the full text of the sermon.

[10] Guillame, ***The Life***, p. 651.

[11] ***Musnad Imam Shafii***

[12] ***Al-Bukhari***, vol. 4, Hadith 660.

[13] Guillame, ***The Life***, p 683.

Does this Essay Cover Any New Ground?

My attempt in this essay has been to study the internal dynamics of Muhammad's ﷺ "struggle," in a holistic manner rather than giving mere details of the events of his life. In essence, it is an analytical, rather than an anecdotal or narrative essay. I have attempted to obtain some insight into his actions during the course of his struggle.

Traditional scholarship's divides his life into Makkan and Madinan phases. This is chronologically valid and represents the two broad aspects of his life before and after the watershed event of the migration. It does not do justice however either to the complexity of his struggle nor reveal its holistic nature. I believe Muhammad's ﷺ struggle can be naturally divided into the seven phases which I have described. Studying the Messenger's ﷺ mission for its various phases is important because it provides precedent and gives the narrative relevance for today. Unlike many of the other messengers in history, Muhammad's ﷺ mission came to a successful end, with many remarkable events in between. Since his life is better documented than the lives of other leaders in the major world religions, it is possible to build this analysis on a historical foundation. When we study the lives of Moses ﷺ (*Musa*), Gautama Buddha, Jesus ﷺ ('*Isa*), and other messianic and charismatic leaders, we cannot help but sense that their stories have many missing chapters.

For instance Moses ﷺ *(Musa)* appears to have constantly struggled to keep his unruly followers in tow. He had trouble keeping them compliant with even the minimum objectives of giving up idol worship and practicing monotheism. The dogmatic concepts, which rankle the outside observer most, are those of the exclusive nature of God (*Yahweh:* the God of the children of Isra'il) and the concept of a chosen community that believes they alone have been elected for redemption. Moses ﷺ (*Musa*) spent his life leading his followers through years of constant wanderings. It was left to

123

his successor Joshua ﷺ to establish a settled structured society. have suffered numerous injustices through the centuries and consequently Jewish thinking appears to have become a captive of their long and often tragic history.

Buddha's mission was also structurally one-dimensional in that it only addresses issues of personal behavior and morality. It does not allow God any role on this earth (Buddhism is non-theistic) nor outline principles for establishing and organizing society. Since Buddha left God's chair vacant, his followers soon enthroned him on it, as the massive statues to Buddha bear witness.

Jesus' ﷺ (*'Isa*) ministry was very brief and in many respects incomplete. Its abrupt end must have left immense confusion and disappointment in the minds of his followers. A number of core theological concepts had not yet become fully clear to those who received his mission during his lifetime, and many different individuals and councils addressed these in later centuries. This may help to explain the controversy, which produced complex concepts like Trinity, which later became central in Christian theology. Although Jesus ﷺ (*'Isa*) left behind a practical precedent in areas of personal behavior, in other areas of community life, such as governance, his followers found few practical examples upon which to rely.

In many areas the contrast between Muhammad's ﷺ struggle and that of the others is dramatic. He began with years of pondering over societal ills. Then came the revelation, and the realization that divine knowledge is essential in guiding the inherently limited human intellect. The profundity of this realization and the enormity of the task ahead of him overawed him. Initially he shared the message only with his closest family and a few loyal supporters.

Next began the phase of proactive change in his mission, and with it the inevitable hostility of the entrenched powers in the society. Change is always threatening, and the greater the change, the more dangerous the threat seems. This would be true of the change against any established system of practices, whether it be economic, social or behavioral. It would also be true for change in personal behavior like wearing immodest clothing, promiscuity, and consumption of intoxicants.

Changing attitudes that valued pride in wealth and country, or class and color of the skin over all else would also be difficult. Often the struggle for change became life threatening. Muhammad ﷺ had to lay his life on the line and on several occasions the mission faced the possibility of total extinction. Fortitude in the face of adversity was the salient feature of this phase.

The migration, which marked the beginning of the next phase, involved careful planning and execution. He demonstrated that self-help and reliance on Allah go together and are both essential for success. With his nomination by the community to a position of leadership, he showed another facet of his personality: the capacity to create a truly pluralistic society with equity and dignity for all religious and ethnic groups.

The period following the migration was consumed by the need to fight wars of survival. However it allowed him to set down exemplary rules of engagement for just warfare: defensive with clear moral objectives; all collateral damage was to be avoided and POWs should be treated humanely; there would be no revenge, and actions would not be motivated by anger. He always led by example and often had to put his own life in danger. These three wars in four years, besides posing a physical threat, must have been extremely distracting and demanding of his time and energy. Yet the work of building the community went on.

During the next phase, he showed the capacity to compromise and demonstrated the foresight and wisdom to realize that peace, even at seemingly unfavorable terms, is better than hostility. The peace dividend, following the treaty with the Quraysh, was huge and resulted in exponential increase in the number of Muslims.

This was followed by the phase of building an exemplary, moral, and just society, a society that functioned in a coherent manner with regard to accumulation and fair distribution of wealth which circulated to even the tiniest capillaries of the community's economic system. It was a pluralistic society with equity and justice for all, governed by mutual consultation, a society based on egalitarianism, equality before the law and protection of its most vulnerable members (women, children, orphans, indigents and slaves).

Then came the conquest of Makkah, which was a demonstration of meticulous planning and the use of overwhelming force to achieve a victory with practically no loss of life on either side of the battle front. The stunning magnanimity and humility shown during victory by Muhammad ﷺ and his companions is unmatched in history. The final sermon, consolidated social, economic, and moral changes that had been brought about in the society. It was time to prepare for the end.

The anatomy of the mission, its growth and evolution in some ways parallels the various stages of human life itself: prenatal (*pre Wahy*), natal and immediate neonatal (*Wahy* and its immediate aftermath), early childhood (open invitation to Islam and brazen hostility), youthful coming of age (new avenues for expansion and migration), young adult life (a clear change in direction of the mission and the major battles), mature middle age (the peace treaty and peace dividend), and finally old age (the completion of his mission). These various stages reflect not only the growing sophistication of the message but also the increasing maturity of the audience to whom the message was directed. The audience also grew in sophistication and in understanding of how to carry the burden of passing on the message. None of this implies that the message was immature, or a work in progress or internally inconsistent at any time.

The Prophet's ﷺ mission was very simply to interpret and spread the Qur'anic ideology. This Qur'an centered spirituality remained the constant theme through all of the phases of his life. The power of the Qur'anic concepts continues to spread even today, making Islam the fastest growing religion in the world. Over time, many differences based on dogma, politics, personality cults and egos have emerged amongst the followers of Islam. In spite of many heterodox sects, the core messages of Qur'an, which are *Tawhid* (every action and thought governed by monotheism in its purest form) and *Taqwa* (personal piety) and the *Jihad* (striving toward the establishment of a just and moral society) are alive and potent, and continue to provide spiritual solace, intellectual satisfaction and societal discipline to many.

Appendices

The Seven Phases of Prophet Muhammad's Life

Appendices

Muhammad's Persona

1. The Qur'an on Muhammad's ﷺ Persona

Indeed there is for you in the Messenger of Allah <u>an excellent pattern</u>.
(Qur'an 33:21)

The Qur'an gives us a glimpse of Muhammad's ﷺ personality in various verses.

With Allah's grace, you behaved with them with a <u>kind heart</u>.
For if you were vengeful or hard hearted, they may have abandoned you.
(Qur'an 3:159)

On another occasion, the Qur'an addresses its listeners in the following fashion,

Among you is a Messenger who <u>is distressed by your difficulties.</u>
He is anxious for your welfare, and is generous towards the believers.
(Qur'an 9:128)

And Muhammad is the bearer of glad tidings and <u>mercy as well as a warner.</u>
And have We not sent you as a mercy unto the worlds.
(Qur'an 21:107)

And have We not sent you but as <u>a bearer of glad tidings and a warner</u> unto all mankind
(Qur'an 34:28)

The Qur'an extols Muhammad's ﷺ high character.

Verily you are of <u>a high and noble character</u>
(Qur'an 68:4)

In addition, it talks about the qualities one would acquire by following him.

Those who follow the Messenger, the unlettered Prophet, whom they find written down in the Torah (Old Testament) and Injil (The book revealed to Jesus)
He bids them to the seemly and prohibits the unseemly;
Allows unto them things clean and forbids unto them things unclean;
And relieves of them of their burden and the shackles which have been upon them.
Those who believe in him and side with him and support him and follow the light which has been sent down with him;
Those shall fare well.
(Qur'an 7:157)

2. Personal Traits (Appearance, Dress, Likes and Dislikes)

Prophet Muhammad ﷺ is reported to have been of medium height, well proportioned with a fair complexion. He had a wide forehead, closely-knit eyebrows, and wide-set black eyes with long eyelashes. His face was lightly fleshy and the mouth was wide. He had a long neck, relatively large head, and broad shoulders. His beard was thick, and his wrists and shoulders were hairy. The palms of his hands were broad and fleshy. The wrists were long, the ankles thin, and the arches of the feet somewhat high. His physical appearance and charisma invariably impressed people. When someone remarked to Jabir bin Samurah that the Prophet's ﷺ face shone like a sword, he replied, "No, it shines like the sun and the moon."

On the Prophet's ﷺ back, between the shoulders, there was a raised oval the size of a pigeon egg. Jabir bin Samurah is quoted in the traditions recorded by both Muslim and Tirmadhi as saying, "I saw a pigeon egg sized raised fleshy area between the Prophet's shoulders." Another description speaks about a collection of moles near the left shoulder, which is sometimes called the seal of the Prophet ﷺ.

His hair was usually shoulder length. At the conquest of Makkah, people noticed his hair was lying on the shoulder in four bundles. As the Prophet ﷺ preferred the "People of the Book" to the *Mushrikun* (disbelievers), and because the *Mushrikun* parted their hair, the Prophet ﷺ initially wore his hair without a part. However, according to Tirmadhi, as later the *Mushrikun* practically disappeared, the Prophet ﷺ no longer felt that he had to be careful not to look like them and started parting his hair. He frequently oiled his hair, and combed it every other day; very few of his hair had turned gray.

The Prophet ﷺ used to walk fast, leaning forward slightly, as if he were walking downhill. His conversation was very sweet and pleasant. He used to speak carefully and in concise sentences so that the listeners often remembered every word of what they had heard. When he wanted to emphasize something, he repeated it several times. Often, when speaking, he appeared to be gazing at the sky.

The most touching description of Muhammad ﷺ is recorded in the words of Khadijah. Consoling him when he was awed and shaken by the first revelation, she said, "Allah will never make you sad. You share the burden of those who have loans they cannot pay, you help the poor, you are a great host, you uphold justice, and you help people in need."

3. Justice

Muhammad ﷺ had an acute sense of justice and fair play. This was seen most clearly when he dealt with his enemies. Once, the body of a companion (Abdullah, cousin of Muhayyisah) was found in a ditch in the town of Khaybar, an exclusively Jewish town. It was clear that he had been murdered. Muhayyisah asked for a judgment of retribution against the people of Khaybar. The Prophet ﷺ asked Muhayyisah if he had witnessed the crime and Muhayyisah replied he had not. However, he suggested that the Jews from Khaybar should be brought in to take an oath that they did not commit the murder. The Prophet ﷺ said that that would be unfair and instead gave the just recompense from the general treasury.

It was common in pagan Arabia for the people from a higher class to be judged by a more lenient standard. Once, a woman from the Quraysh was caught stealing, and one of the companions requested leniency because she was from the tribe of Quraysh. Muhammad's ﷺ face showed signs of some anger. He said, "Banu Isra'il were ruined because they were tough in punishing the poor and were lenient toward the rich."

4. Simplicity and Egalitarianism

Muhammad ﷺ ate anything that was offered to him, so long it was within the bounds of what had been prescribed as acceptable in Islam. He wore anything that was available. Frequently, his clothes were old and rough. In fact, he disliked fancy clothes and formality. He sat down anywhere on the floor, whether on a reed mattress or the bare floor. He frequently wrapped himself in a woolen blanket and sometimes slept in it. His mattress was an animal skin stuffed with date bark. He felt no hesitation or embarrassment in helping with household chores.

The rich and the poor, the free and the slave, the Quraysh and the non-Quraysh were treated alike. Food was shared equally, manual labor (as in the construction of the Masjid at Madinah and the digging of the trench) was shared equally, and above all, justice was meted out equally.

5. Generosity

The Prophet ﷺ could never say no to a request. Once, when someone asked for his help, he replied, "I have nothing to give this time." He then went with that person to 'Umar's house to get the needed help. Many a time, he purchased something from a person and gave it back to the same individual as a donation. He disliked keeping any "*dinar*" (gold coins) for more than three days. At the time of his death, he was practically destitute by choice. Despite his position in the society, he lived a simple and modest life without any luxuries.

6. Attitude Toward the Disenfranchised, the Displaced, the Dispossessed and the Disabled

Although the Qur'an never explicitly banned slavery, Muhammad ﷺ did everything possible by word and action to get rid of it. Freeing a slave was considered an act of high charity. Slaves were allowed to buy their own freedom, and they were to be treated like family members. He would encourage people to use phrases like "my son" and "my child" when referring to slaves. The attitude that slaves were to be treated like family members explains the curious and unique phenomenon of slave kings and rulers in Muslim history. Both in India and Egypt, kings nominated their favorite slave to succeed them to the throne, resulting in slave dynasties of kings which lasted several generations.

Another group of abused and dispossessed in the society was women. He was able to achieve dramatic changes in the status of women. I will discuss the issue in some detail later.

7. A Gracious Host

Muhammad ﷺ took great pleasure in personally serving his guests. It was not uncommon for him to serve whatever he had at home and let his family go hungry. He liked giving gifts and was also pleased to accept them. "Send each other gifts. It will increase love and affection."

However, he would not accept favors. When Abu Bakr gave him a camel for the ride during *Hijrah* (Migration), he paid Abu Bakr for it. Even the land on which the first Masjid was built in Madinah was not accepted without compensating its owner.

8. Dislike of Begging, Monastic Behavior and Excessive Praise

The Prophet Muhammad ﷺ is recorded as saying, "It is better to carry wood on your back and sell it, than beg." On another occasion, he said, "On the day of reckoning, begging will be like a blemish on the face of the beggar."

He said begging is permitted in three extreme situations. First, for someone who is literally drowning in debt, he may beg until his needs are met. Second, when someone is affected by a sudden financial tragedy, he may beg until he is back on his feet. Third, if someone is starving he may beg.

Some of Muhammad's ﷺ companions considered adopting monastic behavior for self-purification and attainment of greater spirituality. When the Prophet ﷺ heard of this, he called them in and expressed his displeasure. He said, "Your body has a right over you, so do your eyes and so does your wife." Some companions would fast daily. He admonished them not to fast for more than three days in a month (except during Ramadan). When one of the companions insisted that he had the strength to fast more often, Muhammad ﷺ allowed him to fast every other day, saying, "This was Dawud's (David) (as) practice."

He particularly disliked excessive praise. When someone would start praising him, he would immediately stop him. On another occasion, when someone started reciting poetry in his praise, he stopped him by saying, "Do not praise me excessively—; I am but a servant of Allah."

9. Promises and Pacts

Muhammad ﷺ always kept his word. The Makkans used to call him *al-Amin* (the trustworthy) even before he received the *Wahy* (revelation). When Negus, the Christian ruler of Ethiopia, was interrogating the Muslims who had migrated to Ethiopia about Muhammad's ﷺ character, one of his questions was, "Does your Messenger keep his word?" The answer was, "Yes; always!" Whether it was the Covenant of Madinah or the Treaty of Hudaybiyah, all pacts were honored scrupulously.

10. Forgiveness

Muhammad ﷺ never took personal revenge and forgave easily and quickly. There are many instances when he took verbal and even physical abuse imperturbably. Sometimes his companions would become very upset at the insulting and arrogant behavior of the Quraysh. He would cool them down and urge them to forgive. He forgave even his worst enemies. His forgiveness and grace toward Hind, on whose urging Hamzah was murdered and mutilated, stands as a witness to his extraordinary compassion. He was always courteous to the *Munafiqun* (hypocrites) and even the pagans (*Kuffar*) in the community. He knew that some of the hypocrites would participate in congregational prayer and even in some battles. He was fully aware of the fact, but never confronted them.

11. Desire To Spread Literacy and Education

Although personally unlettered he loved education. The acquisition and spread of knowledge was considered a sacred duty. He frequently ransomed prisoners of war if they promised to teach Muslims to read and write. "The ink in a scholar's pen," he is reported to have said, "is more precious than the blood of a martyr."

12. Public Display of Affection

He was a very affectionate man and had no hesitation in displaying it. Whenever he met Fatimah, his daughter, he would greet her very warmly. This love for her daughter was not tainted by even a trace of favoritism.

Because of all the hard manual work Fatimah had to do at home, like carrying water from the well in the "*mishk*" (water skin) and using a hand mill to crush grain into flour, her hands had black and blue marks and calluses. Yet, Muhammad ﷺ would not allot her a servant. They were allotted preferentially to those who fought in the battle of Badr.

13. Humor

Muhammad ﷺ liked humor. He smiled a lot and enjoyed playing with children. There are multiple examples of his gentle sense of humor.

Once, an old woman came up to him and asked for paradise. He said, "Old women do not enter the paradise." The woman started crying. As she started leaving the room, the

Prophet ﷺ, showing his subtle sense of humor, stopped her and said, "Old women will become young before entering the heaven." (Tirmadhi)

One of his companions was Zahir, who used to trade in metal objects. Once the Prophet ﷺ was passing by the bazaar, he saw Zahir and playfully grabbed him from behind and said, "Will anyone buy this slave?" Zahir laughed and said, "O Messenger of Allah, whoever buys this slave will be in loss." The Prophet ﷺ smiled and said, "In Allah's eyes, your value is high."

On another occasion, a man approached the Prophet ﷺ and asked him for a camel to ride. The Prophet ﷺ said, "I would give you a camel's child." The man said, "O Messenger of Allah. What will I do with a camel's child?" The Prophet ﷺ smiled and said, "Is there any camel who is not the progeny of a camel?"

Studying reports in *Sirah* (biography of the Prophet ﷺ) and Hadith literature, Muhammad's ﷺ personality emerges as that of a thoughtful, introspective individual, who lived a modest life. He was easily accessible to even the poorest in the community, disliked excesses in behavior, had a gentle sense of humor, was profoundly God conscious, and was single-mindedly devoted to establishing socio-economic justice.

The defamous image created by some authors of a man who was cunning, cruel, unjust, power hungry, and given to debauchery is such a fiction that it must astound any serious scholar of Muhammad's ﷺ life. In fact, upon reviewing the biographical literature of religious leaders, it is difficult to come up with another example in which a religious or world leader has been so misrepresented, vilified and calumniated.

Appendices

The Prophet's Marriages and Wives

One line of hostile argument against Islam and the Prophet ﷺ begins in the following manner: he married multiple times, which proves he was a voluptuary! The argument then goes on to conclude that any serious study of the religion of which this licentious person was the primary spokesperson would be worthless.

Even a cursory examination of Muhammad's ﷺ marriages however destroys these widely held myths. I will list Muhammad's ﷺ marriages in chronological order and describe the rationale and circumstances surrounding them.

1. Khadijah bint Khuwaylid

Khadijah, his first wife, was a widow who was much older than Muhammad ﷺ when she proposed to him. Because of her success in business and lineage, many of the wealthy among the Quraysh desired to marry her. She, however, was impressed by Muhammad's ﷺ character and so she initiated the marriage proposal. She was his steadfast supporter in extremely trying times and always provided wise counsel and solace. She was the first person to accept Islam. Khadijah died approximately twenty-five years after they married, and Prophet Muhammad ﷺ continued to revere her memory for the rest of his life.

2. Sawdah bint Zam'ah

After Khadijah's death, the Prophet married Sawdah. She was also a widow. She and her husband had accepted Islam very early in the mission and had been among the migrants to Ethiopia. She was a tall and rather heavyset individual. She was also very well known for her charity.

The marriage of Muhammad ﷺ to Sawdah set the trend of the Prophet ﷺ marrying widows of Muslims who had died of natural causes or during one of the many battles. The social structure of the time was not conducive for widows or women living singly. One could argue that today, in societies like Bosnia and Chechnya, where large members of men have become the victims of genocide, multiple marriages to widows would be a reasonable remedy for these women living in dire poverty and destitution, or turning to prostitution to survive.

3. 'Aishah bint Abu Bakr

It was customary in the Arab society for close friendships and bonds to be strengthened by marriage into the family. Muhammad ﷺ married the daughters of his two closest associates, Abu Bakr as-Siddiq and 'Umar ibn al-Khattab, the first two Khalifahs (successors of the Prophet ﷺ) of Islam. In turn, three of the daughters of the Prophet ﷺ were married to the other two companions who became the third and fourth Khalifahs, Uthman ibn 'Affan and 'Ali ibn Abu Talib.

The youngest of his wives, 'Aishah, Abu Bakr's daughter, was a remarkable woman. Her lively personality comes through in the quotes attributed to her in the *Sirah* and Hadith literature. Muhammad ﷺ took permission from his other wives and spent the last days of his life with her and he died in her arms. She was extremely intelligent and erudite. Much of the stronger Hadith literature is attributed to her. Many of the companions would seek her help in resolving difficult legal problems.

4. Hafsah bint 'Umar

When Hafsah became a widow, her father 'Umar, one of the great Khalifahs of Islam, started looking for a husband for her. He initially asked Uthman. Uthman's wife, Ruqayyah, one of the Prophet's ﷺ daughters, had just died. However Uthman demurred. 'Umar then asked Abu Bakr to marry her, but Abu Bakr also declined. He then finally asked Muhammad ﷺ. Sensing what was going on, the Prophet ﷺ readily agreed.

Later when during Uthman's caliphate the authoritative version of the Qur'an was redacted Hafsah would be the custodian of the manuscript.

5. Zaynab bint Khuzaymah (The Mother of the Indigent)

Zaynab's husband 'Ubaydah was killed in the battle of Badr. Muhammad ﷺ immediately offered to marry her. She had the reputation of being extremely caring toward the needy and the indigent. She was known as *Umm al-Masakin* (The mother of the poor). She died within two or three months of her marriage to the Prophet ﷺ.

6. Umm Salamah bint Abu Umayyah

Her real name was Hind, but she was known as Umm Salamah. Her husband, Abdullah bin Abdul Asad was known as Abu Salamah. They had migrated to Ethiopia, and Abu Salamah was well known for his courage and prowess as an equestrian. He died from injuries sustained during the battle of Uhud. Umm Salamah was pregnant at that time. After waiting the required period, Muhammad ﷺ proposed marriage to her. She initially refused, citing reasons of being old and having children from the previous marriage, but Muhammad ﷺ insisted.

She was with Muhammad ﷺ during the trip to Makkah from the pilgrimage, which resulted in the Hudaybiyah treaty. Her advice and counsel proved crucial during those very critical days.

7. Zaynab bint Jahsh

Zaynab had been married to Zayd bin Thabit. Zayd was Muhammad's ﷺ slave before the advent of Islam. Muhammad ﷺ appeared to set a precedent that slaves should be freed and should carry no stigma from their past. Zaynab, who was Muhammad's ﷺ cousin, may have married Zayd under moral duress. The exact rationale behind the marriage is unclear. The marriage did not last long. It is possible that the Prophet ﷺ felt some responsibility about the failed marriage and therefore the necessity to marry her.

The Qur'an offers an additional explanation for the marriage. Two of the prevalent customs in the society were to banish "wives" into limbo by declaring them to be their husband's "mothers," (as discussed earlier, the practice was called *Zihar*), and to declare foster children as one's natural children. The Prophet's ﷺ marriage to Zaynab, who was divorced from Zayd, abolished the latter practice. Zaynab was known for her extraordinary piety and righteousness. She was in her late middle age when she married the Prophet ﷺ.

8. Juwariyah bint al-Harith

The prisoners of war captured after the defeat of Banu Musta'liq (sub-tribe of Khuza'ah) included Juwayriyah. She was the daughter of the defeated tribal chief. Her husband had been killed in the skirmish. She would have become a companion's, Thabit bin Qays', slave. She found that unacceptable and petitioned the Prophet ﷺ. He freed her by paying Thabit her ransom and offered to restore her prestige by marrying her. She accepted, and an important by-product of the marriage was that the entire over seven hundred prisoners of war of the tribe of Banu Musta'liq were freed.

9. Umm Habibah bint Abu Sufyan

Ramla (mother of Habibah) was initially married to 'Ubaydullah bin Jahsh. The two migrated to Ethiopia, and after the migration 'Ubaydullah converted to Christianity. Ramla remained a Muslim, resulting in a separation and divorce. Muhammad ﷺ sent an envoy to Negus with a proposal that he should conduct his marriage to Umm Habibah "in absentia."

10. Safiyyah bint Huyay

Her real name was Zaynab, but she was known by the nickname of Safiyyah. She was a prisoner of war following an assault on Khaybar. Both her father and brother had died during the war. She was initially assigned to a companion, Wahyi Kalby, but when it was realized that she was the daughter of a tribal chief, other companions objected.

11. Maymunah bint al-Harith

Maymunah's first marriage resulted in a divorce, and her second husband died, making her both a widow and a divorcee. One of the Prophet's close companions, Abbas proposed that Muhammad should marry her. He agreed, demonstrating that it was no longer a stigma for a woman to be both divorced and widowed. They felt it would be inappropriate for her to be assigned to anyone other than the Prophet. She was occasionally the subject of sarcasm because of her Jewish parentage. Whenever the Prophet became aware of this, he showed his annoyance.

12. Mariyah

Muhammad's last son was born to Mariyah, the Coptic. She was one of the two slave girls presented to the Prophet by the Archbishop of Alexandria. She gave birth to a son, Ibrahim, who, like the other two sons born to Khadijah, died in infancy.

The Rationale behind the Prophet's Marriages.

The rationale behind these marriages is clear. Many were performed to rehabilitate divorced and widowed women, especially widows of companions who had been killed in the early battles. Sometimes, Muhammad had to go to great lengths to persuade the women to marry him. Other marriages were done to strengthen bonds between friends and tribes. Some were done as an act of compassion toward a conquered foe.

In the society of those times, they were regarded as acts of nobility and kindness. With the exception of the marriage to Zaynab bint Jahsh, none appeared to create any controversy. The controversy surrounding Zaynab's marriage soon dissipated as the motive behind it became clear.

All of his wives distinguished themselves in some area of charity, kindness, or erudition and knowledge (as in the case of 'Aishah). They were held to a higher standard and were informed that both their rewards and punishments were greater than for other women in the society. The Qur'an honors them as the "Mothers of the believers". Their marriages to the Prophet ﷺ were voluntary and they could initiate and ask for divorce if they so desired.

The Qur'an and Muhammad ﷺ made revolutionary changes in the status of women and his wives were in many ways exemplars of these changes. As the Prophet's ﷺ dealings with his wives were based on love, affection, respect and dignity, others in the society were expected to follow his exemplary behavior. Men and women were declared equal in the eyes of Allah ﷻ. Compassion, equity, and justice were mandated. Rules were laid down for marriage and divorce. Laws regarding ownership of property were promulgated. The notion of the moral superiority of men over women was shot down. Men were told that they had the duty to protect women and children. As mentioned earlier, the Qur'an stresses the moral and spiritual equality of men and women in emphatic and unambiguous language.[1]

---

[1] Qur'an 33:35.

Appendices

The Covenant of Madinah

In the name of Allah the Compassionate, the Merciful

This is a document from Muhammad the Prophet (governing the relations) between the Muslims of the Quraysh and Madinah, and their allies who would follow them and fight with them.

1. They are one community (*Ummah*) to the exclusion of all men.

2. The Quraysh emigrants, according to their present custom, shall pay just recompense within their numbers and shall redeem their prisoners with kindness and justice, common among believers.

3. The Banu 'Awf according to their custom shall pay the just recompense they paid in heathenism: every section shall redeem its prisoners with the kindness and justice, common among believers.

4-10. The Banu Sa'idah (clan of Khazraj) and the Banu al-Harith, and the Banu Jusham, and the Banu an-Najjar likewise. The Banu 'Amr (clan of Aws), the Banu al-Nabit and the Banu al-Aws likewise.

11. The believers shall not leave anyone destitute among them by not paying his redemption money or just recompense in kindness.

12. A believer shall not take as an ally (*mawla*) the freedman of another Muslim against him.

13. The Allah-fearing believers shall be against the rebellious or him who seeks to spread injustice, or sin or enmity or corruption between believers; the hand of every man shall be against him, even if he were a son of one of them.

14. A believer shall not slay a believer, nor shall he aid an unbeliever against a believer.

15. Allah's obligation is uniform for all. The weakest among the believers can grant protection to another and make it obligatory for all believers to honor his protection. Believers are friends to one another to the exclusion of outsiders.

16. To the Jew who is an ally belong help and equality. He shall not be wronged nor shall his enemies be aided.

17. The peace of the believers is indivisible. No separate peace shall be made when believers are fighting in the path of Allah, until the peace is equitable to all.

18. In every foray all groups will be behind each other (support each other)

19. The believers must avenge the blood of another shed in the way of Allah.

20. The Allah-fearing believers enjoy the best and the most upright guidance.

21. A polytheist shall not take the property or person of Quraysh under his protection, nor shall he intervene against a believer.

22. The killing a believer without good reason, as proven by reliable witnesses, shall be subject to retaliation unless the next of kin are satisfied (with just recompense). The believers shall be against him as one man, and they are bound to act against him and convict him regardless of who he is.

23. It shall not be lawful to a believer who holds what is in the document and believes in Allah and the last day to help an evildoer or to shelter him. If he does so, the curse of Allah and His anger on the day of resurrection will be upon him and neither repentance nor ransom will be received from him.

24. Whenever you differ about a matter it must be referred to Allah and to Muhammad.

25. The Jews shall contribute to the cost of war so long as they are fighting alongside the believers.

26. The Jews of Banu 'Awf are one community with the believers (the Jews have their religion and the Muslims have theirs) and their freedmen, except those who behave unjustly and sinfully, for they hurt but themselves and their families.

27-36. The same applies to Jews of the Banu an-Najjar, Banu al-Harith, Banu Sa'idah, Banu Jusham, Banu al-Aws, Banu Tha'labah and the Jafna clan of the Tha'labah, and the Banu al-Shutayba. Loyalty is a protection against treachery. The same applies to the freedmen of Tha'labah and the close friends of Jews.

37. None of them shall go out to war save with the permission of Muhammad.

38. He shall not be prevented from taking revenge for an injury. He who slays a man without warning slays himself and his household, unless it be one who has wronged him, for Allah will accept that.

39. The Jews must bear their expenses and Muslims theirs.

40. Each must help the other against anyone who attacks the people of this document. They shall seek mutual advice and consultation, and loyalty is a protection against treachery.

41. A man is not liable for his ally's misdeeds. The wronged must be helped.

42. The Jews must pay with the believers so long as the war lasts.

43. Madinah shall be a sanctuary for people of this document.

44. A stranger under protection shall be as his host. He will not be harmed and no crime will be committed against him.

45. A woman shall be not given protection without the consent of her family.

46. If any dispute or controversy likely to cause trouble should arise it must be referred to Allah and to Muhammad the Apostle of Allah. Allah accepts what is nearest to piety and goodness in this document.

47. Quraysh and their helpers shall not be given protection.

48. The contracting parties are bound to help one another against any attack on Madinah.

49. If they are called to make peace and maintain it they must do so; and if they make a similar demand on the Muslims it must be carried out except in the case of a war to protect *Din*.[1] *(Haaraab fi ad-Din)*

50. Everyone shall defend whom he is faced with.

51. The Jews of al-Aws and their freedmen and themselves have the same standing with the people of this document.

52. This deed will not protect the unjust and the sinner. The man who goes forth to fight and the man who stays at home in the city are safe unless he has been unjust and has sinned.

53. God is the protector of the good and the Allah-fearing; and Muhammad is his Apostle; Allah is his ally.

---

[1] The Arabic word *Din* has a broader meaning than religion. The Qur'an uses it to denote "exclusive obedience to Allah" (Lo! For Allah is exclusive obedience. Qur'an, 39:3) as well as "judgment". (The owner of the day of judgment. Qur'an, 1:3)

Appendices

The Treaty of Hudaybiyah

This is what Muhammad ibn Abdullah has agreed with Suhayl ibn 'Amr:

They have agreed to lay aside war for ten years during which men can be safe and refrain from hostilities on condition that:

If anyone comes to Muhammad without the permission of his guardian, he will return him to them;

And if anyone of those with Muhammad comes to Quraysh, they will not return him to him (Muhammad);

We will not show enmity one to another and there shall be no secret reservation or bad faith;

He who wishes to enter into a bond or agreement with Muhammad may do so;

And he who wishes to enter into a bond or agreement with Quraysh may do so;

You (Muslims) must retire from us this year and not enter Makkah against our will;

And next year we will make way for you and you can carry a riders weapons, the swords in their sheath. You can bring in nothing more.

Appendices

Prophet Muhammad's Letter to Heraclius[1]

In the name of Allah the Beneficent and the Merciful.

(This letter) is from Muhammad, the servant of Allah and His Messenger to Heraclius, the ruler of Byzantine.
Peace be upon him who follows the right path.
Further more I invite you to Islam and if you become a Muslim you will be safe, and Allah will double your reward and if you reject this invitation, you will be committing a sin by misguiding your *arisiyin* (subjects). (And I recite to you Allah's statement)

O people of the scripture! Come to a word common to you and us that we worship none but Allah and that we associate nothing in worship with Him and none of us shall take others as Lords besides Allah. Then if they turn away say: bear witness that we are Muslims.
(Qur'an 3:64)

---

[1] ***al-Bukhari***, The Book of Revelation, vol. 1.

Appendices

Said the Messenger of Allah...[1]

These are some of the examples of Muhammad's ﷺ prayers and words as recorded in the Hadith literature.

1. O Allah! Improve my spiritual life, for that is to be my refuge;
   And purify my material life, for I have to live it;
   And prepare me for the life to which I shall have to return;
   And keep me alive till it is good for me to be alive,
   And call me back when it is good for me to die.
   And lengthen my life in every goodly state,
   And turn death into bliss before any evil state supervenes.
   (Hisn-al-Hisn)

2. The believer is not he who eats his full, while his neighbor is hungry.
   (Bayhaqi)

3. Food for two is sufficient for three, and food for three is sufficient for four.
   (Muslim)

4. Give the laborer his wages before his sweat dries.
   (Ibn Majah)

5. He who unjustly takes land measuring but a hand-span will have sevenfold the measure of that land hung around his neck.
   (Bukhari-Muslim)

6. Four traits of a hypocrite are:
   He betrays a trust, lies, breaks promises, and when he quarrels, he commits excesses.
   (Bukhari)

7. Beware of envy, for envy devours good (deeds) like fire devours firewood.
(Abu Dawud)

8. Beware of suspicion, for suspicion is the greatest falsehood.
Do not try to find fault in each other; do not spy on one another,
Do not vie with one another; do not envy one another,
Do not be angry with one another,
And be servants of Allah ﷺ, brothers to one another, as you have been enjoined.
A Muslim is the brother of a Muslim - he does him no wrong, nor does he let him down; nor does he despise him. Fear of Allah ﷺ is here, fear of Allah ﷺ is here.
It is evil for a Muslim should look down on his brother.
For every Muslim is sacred to another - his blood, his honor and his property.
Allah does not look at your bodies, your forms, or your deeds, but he looks at your hearts.
(Bukhari and Muslim)

9. Charity is due upon every limb of a human being on each day that the sun rises. To act justly between two (people) is charity. To help a man to his riding beast, or to load his provisions on it or lift them up for him is charity. A good word is charity. Every step going to prayer is charity. Removing from the road what causes harm is charity.
(Bukhari, Muslim)

10. One, who strives to strengthen an oppressor and knows he is an oppressor, has already left Islam. (Bayhaqi)

11. If one of you sees (something) bad, he should change it with his hand; and if he is not capable of that, then with his tongue; and if he is not capable of that, then with his heart, and that is the weakest faith.
(Muslim)

12. Leave what you have doubt about for that you have no

doubt about; for it is truth that brings peace of mind and it is falsehood that brings doubt.
(Musnad Ahmad, Tirmadhi and Nasai}

13. The strong man is not the one who is strong in wrestling, but the one who controls his anger.

14. A companion asked "O Messenger of Allah! What do you fear most for me?" Thereupon he pointed at his own tongue and said, "This."
(Tirmadhi)

15. 'Do you know backbiting?'
They said, 'Allah and His messenger know best.'
He said, '(When) you speak about your brother, what he would dislike it is backbiting.'
Someone said, 'What if my brother is as I say?'
He said, 'If he is as you say, you have been backbiting; and if he is not as you say, you have slandered him.'
(Muslim)

16. The Muslim who meets with people and endures any harm they may do, is better than he who does not meet with them and does not endure any harm they may do.
(Tirmadhi)

17. Allah ﷻ is not merciful to him who is not merciful to his people.
(Bukhari, Muslim)

18. He who does not thank people does not thank Allah ﷻ.
(Musnad Ahmad and Tirmadhi)

19. When a man loves his brother (for the sake of Allah ﷻ) he should tell him that he loves him.
(Abu Dawud and Tirmadhi)

20. Some of the companions reported that, Allah's Messenger ﷺ came out leaning on a stick and we stood up. He said: "Do not stand up as the foreigners stand up exalting each other therewith."
(Abu Dawud)

21. Visit the sick, feed the hungry and free the captives.
(Bukhari)

22. Do not withhold *(Sadaqah)* or Allah ﷻ withholds you. Give away whatever you can afford.
(Bukhari)

23. According to 'Aishah: Allah's Messenger ﷺ used to receive gifts and used to give (gifts).
(Bukhari)

24. The best companion with Allah ﷻ is he who behaves best to his companions and the best neighbor to Allah ﷻ is he who behaves best to his neighbor.
(Tirmadhi)

25. He who believes in Allah ﷻ and the Last Day should honor his guests according to his right. People asked, "What is his right, Messenger of Allah?" He said, "A day and a night, and hospitality for three days. And beyond that is *Sadaqah*."
(Bukhari and Muslim)

26. The most perfect of the believers is the best of you in character; and the best of you are those among you who are best to their wives.
(Tirmadhi)

27. He is not of us who has no compassion for our little ones and does not honor our old ones.
(Abu Dawud and Tirmadhi)

28. The best house among Muslims is the house in which an orphan is well treated and the worst house among the Muslims is the house in which an orphan is badly treated. (Ibn Majah)

29. Each of you is a guardian, and each of you will be asked about your guardianship. The leader is a guardian, the man is a guardian over the people of his house, and the woman is a guardian over her husband's house and children. So each of you is a guardian, and each of you will be asked about your guardianship. (Bukhari and Muslim)

30. Go back to your people and teach them. (Bukhari)

31. Make things easy, do not make them difficult, and give good tiding and do not make people run away. (Bukhari)

Say! Verily, my prayer and my sacrifice and my life and death are for Allah.
(Qur'an 6:162)

---

[1] Most of the sayings are taken from Ahmad Von Denffer, *A Day with the Prophet.* (Leicester, UK: Islamic Foundation, 1979).

Appendices

The Sermon at the Last Pilgrimage

This Sermon was delivered on the Ninth Day of Dhul Hijjah 10 A.H in the Uranah Valley of mount 'Arafat

"O People, lend me an attentive ear, for I do not know whether, after this year, I shall ever be amongst you again. Therefore listen to what I am saying to you carefully and take these words to those who could not be present here today.

O People, just as you regard this month, this day, this city as Sacred, so regard the life and property of every Muslim as a sacred trust. Return the goods entrusted to you to their rightful owners. Hurt no one so that no one may hurt you. Remember that you will indeed meet your Lord, and that He will indeed reckon your deeds. Allah has forbidden you to take usury, therefore all usurious obligation shall henceforth be waived.

Beware of Satan, for the safety of your religion. He has lost all hope that he will ever be able to lead you astray in big things, so beware of following him in small things.

O People, it is true that you have certain rights concerning your women, but they also have rights over you. If they abide by your rights then to them belongs the right to be fed and clothed in kindness. Do treat your women well and be kind to them for they are your partners and committed helpers. Moreover, it is your right that they do not make friends with any one of whom you do not approve, as well as never commit adultery.

O People, listen to me in earnest, worship Allah, say your five daily prayers (*Salah*), fast during the month of Ramadan, and give your wealth in *Zakat*. Perform the Hajj if you can afford to. You know that every Muslim is the brother of another Muslim. You are all equal. Nobody has superiority over other except by piety and good action.

Remember, one day you will appear before Allah and answer for your deeds. So beware! Do not astray from the path of righteousness after I am gone.

O People! No prophet or apostle will come after me and no new faith will be born. Reason well, therefore, O People! And understand my words that I convey to you. I leave behind me two things, the Qur'an and my example, the Sunnah and if you follow these you will never go astray.

All those who listen to me shall pass on my words to others and those to others again; and the last ones may understand my words better than those who listen to me directly may. Be my witness Oh Allah! that I have conveyed your message to the people."

Appendices

The Satanic Verses?

The "Satanic verses" need to be mentioned only because of the notoriety they have gained recently because of the Salman Rushdie affair. It was alleged that Muhammad ﷺ, in a spirit of compromise, implicitly accepted the worship of old pagan idols, Lat, 'Uzza and Manat. According to some accounts he used the word "Gharaniq" to describe the Qurayshi idols. The term Gharaniq means, "Numidian cranes" which fly at great heights, and is a laudatory term. It is inconceivable that Muhammad ﷺ would compromise on the issue of monotheism. In fact some of his followers had already died rather than admit to Shirk (associating anything else with Allah ﷻ). *Tawhid*, described best as pure Monotheism without any associates or even subsidiary deities, is at the core of Islam. Every Qur'anic verse is suffused and illuminated with the concept of *Tawhid*, which is at once both intimidating and liberating. Some of the scholars who chronicled the words and deeds of Muhammad ﷺ (*Hadith* and *Sirah*), notably at-Tabari and Ibn Ishaq, considered it plausible and recorded this incident while most others, including Bukhari and Muslim, believed that the narrators (*rawis*) were not trustworthy and rejected it.

Still others provide an alternative explanation. The Quraysh would frequently crowd around Muhammad ﷺ and speak noisily to try to interfere with the public recitation of the Qur'an near the Ka'bah. When Muhammad ﷺ recited, *"Have you ever given a thought to Lat and 'Uzza, and Manat, the third (idol)"*[1] someone may have shouted, "Lat and 'Uzza and the third Manat, they are the exalted Gharaniq, whose intercession is approved." The Quraysh commonly used this invocation during the circumambulation of the Ka'bah while performing the pre-Islamic pilgrimage.

The Qur'an itself records the following verses which follows the previous verses more naturally

What! Shall ye assign to yourselves the males and to Him the females.
(Qur'an 53:21)

These three verses are a pointed comment on the hypocrisy in the Qurayshi society that treated women as chattel and yet had female deities as its major idols and has nothing to do with any Satanic interdiction in the revelatory process. Muslim outrage at Rushdie was the result of the knowledge that the statements in his book were maliciously slanderous and their only discernible intent in distorting the account was to cause deliberate provocation and blasphemy.

---

[1] Qur'an 53:19-20.

Appendices

The Quintessentials of the Islamic Belief System

Muslims believe in one transcendental God, *Allah*. The belief in one God is called *Tawhid*. The Arabic word Allah is unique, as it has no derivatives. It is neither plural nor gender specific; thus it emphasizes that the one and only God is neither male nor female. Allah's omnipotence and omnipresence transcend time, space and gender.

While acknowledging many of the prophets of the Old Testament, and having as an article of faith the belief that every nation in history had its own warner and messenger, Muslims believe that Muhammad was the final Prophet of God. They acknowledge the prophethood but not the divinity of 'Isa (Jesus). They are very careful not to attribute any divinity to Muhammad either, and in doing so they feel they are fulfilling his wishes to be remembered as a human and not an angelic or otherworldly being. Muslims believe in the eternal message of their scripture, the Qur'an, and the historical and theological relationship of other related scriptures, especially the Old Testament and the Bible. The Qur'an was revealed to Muhammad in segments of varying lengths over a twenty-three year period and remains unchanged today fourteen hundred years later.

Muslims believe in individual accountability and responsibility. All humans start with a clean record and with the freedom to chose between right, the *halal,* and wrong, the *haram.* They are answerable to their own deeds without any intermediary between them and God. Through the Qur'an, mankind is the recipient of divine knowledge and wisdom. Knowledge is glorified in Islam. The first word revealed to the prophet Muhammad was *Iqra*' (recite). The acquiring, spreading, and expanding of knowledge is considered a sacred duty. Muslims remind themselves of their obligation to God by worshipping (*salah*) five times a day, which forms part of their obligation to God or '*Ibadat,* which primarily deal with the hereafter.

Their obligations to other humans, which affect life here on this earth, are called *Mu'amalat* (civil transactions). Like many other faiths, Islam believes in devotion to parents, goodwill, kindness, forgiveness towards others and self-restraint. The practice of self-restraint however is not to be interpreted as sanctioning or encouraging monasticism. Although there are many examples of individual Muslims who were celibate throughout their lives, it is recommended that individuals marry and that they fully participate in the joys and trials of life on this earth. The institution of marriage is at the core of Muslim family life. A Muslim marriage is a contract rather than a sacrament. Civility between spouses is mandated by the Qur'an and reinforced by the Prophet's ﷺ own life. In case of marital discord, arbitration and counseling is highly recommended. Divorce is permitted only as a last resort.

The same principles that govern private conduct between individuals also govern societies. The use of alcohol and drugs is forbidden since they are both personal addictions, which are harmful to the society. Gambling enterprises, including state lotteries, are forbidden. Personal piety is reinforced by the practice of self-restraint and self-denial all during the ninth month of the lunar calendar (*Ramadan*). This exercise in reinvigorating personal piety by fasting, *Sawm*, is also a unique public event in which the whole community participates.

Justice is another value that Islam places at the core of a healthy and peaceful society. The Prophet Muhammad ﷺ exhorted his followers to stop injustice actively or at the very least not to rationalize it. In extreme cases of injustice, Muslims have the right of self-defense. To struggle against an unjust cause or personal temptation is referred to as *Jihad*, which is not equivalent of holy war. *Jihad* in the deepest sense is the eternal struggle in human life between good and evil forces.

Principles of justice and equality also govern gender and race relations. Men and women are equal in the eyes of Allah ﷻ. Religious responsibilities are largely the same for men and women; each must pray, fast, give alms and go on pilgrimage to Makkah. While men and women are seen as being equal, they are also seen as having distinct and complementary roles.

Modesty of clothing and behavior is encouraged for both men and women. The intent is to create an environment in which the spiritual rather than the sensual qualities of men and women are given prominence. Over time, this idea has been corrupted by various cultural forces and has been made to appear as religious sanction for discrimination against women. The concept of equality applies to all classes and races. A dramatic example of this is seen during the Muslim pilgrimage to Makkah called the *Hajj,* where all Muslims, rich and poor, black and white, wear the same clothing as a sign of universal brotherhood. This concept of racial equality is one of the most deeply rooted principles of Islam.

The egalitarianism and emphasis on human dignity carry into the notion of self-respect and freedom from blasphemy and false accusations. In Islamic Shari'ah law the penalty for bringing a false accusation is as severe as the alleged crime. Human rights are an original Islamic concept. European crusaders learned the principles of humane treatment of prisoners of war from their contact with Islamic jurisprudence.

Muslim jurisprudence is based on the rights and principles called the *Shari'ah.* Individuals have a right to life, dignity, family, knowledge, property, and freedom from coercion in matters of religion. Crimes are regarded as violations of divine not human law. Islamic punishments (*Hudud*) have received much criticism for being harsh. These punishments are effective because they are tempered by a fastidiously fair judicial process and by compassion, forgiveness and a general God-consciousness in the society. Even in the case of death penalty for murder, relatives of the victim are encouraged to forgive and accept fair restitution. Islam believes strongly in the sanctity of human life and does not allow for its destruction, including suicide and most cases of abortion.

In Islamic law, the right to own property and generate wealth is tempered by an acute sense of fair dealing, equitable distribution of wealth and socioeconomic justice. One of the main tenets of Islam is *Zakat,* a compulsory sharing of wealth with needy members of the society. A productive economy free of exploitation is required and encouraged. Concerning the public polity, Islam stipulates only the guiding principles of "government by the righteous" and "governance by consultation'. No specific government structure is recommended, a fact which has resulted in a wide spectrum of political systems. As Islam is a holistic belief system so there is no separation between religion and governance.

The richness and rectitude of the Islamic belief system is designed to enhance the social, economic and moral fiber of the society. For a few glorious years it did accomplish that ideal and has the potential to do so if the followers of Islam choose to practice it with sincerity.

Primary Sources

1. Qur'an as a source of the Sirah

The Qur'an itself provides the most interesting and objective source of the Prophet's ﷺ *Sirah*. He is mentioned directly only four times (in contrast, the name *Musa* ﷺ (Moses) appears one hundred and twenty seven times and *Isa* ﷺ (Jesus) twenty five times). However, the entire Qur'an, in a way, is addressed to him. Multiple indirect references to events in the Prophet's ﷺ life and mission abound. Most fascinating of all, is that the Qur'an is occasionally critical of the Prophet ﷺ and gently chides him. A striking example is in the Surat 'Abasa.

> *(The Prophet) frowned and turned away*
> *Because there came to him the blind man*
> *However, what could tell thee but perchance that he might grow (in spiritual understanding)*
> *Or that he might receive admonition and the teachings profit him?*
> *As to the one who regards himself as self-sufficient*
> *To him dost thou attend?*
> *Though it is no blame to thee if he grows not (in spiritual understanding)*
> *But as to him who came to thee striving earnestly*
> *And with fear in his heart*
> *Of him wast thou unmindful!*
> *By no means (shouldst it be so)!*
> *For it is indeed a message of instruction.*
> *(Qur'an 80:1-11)*

I have tried to include many but not all of these Qur'anic references to Muhammad's ﷺ life.

2. Ibn Ishaq (born AH 85/died AH 151)

This is the major source of Muhammad's ﷺ life. There were at least seven other attempts at documenting *Sirah*. None of them survived. 'Uqbah's (55-141 AH) Sirah of the Prophet

ﷺ, which was one of those seven books was endorsed by Malik ibn Anas, Idris al- Shafi'i, and Ahmad ibn Hanbal, did not survive.

A pupil of Ibn Ishaq made two copies of his manuscript. One reached Ibn Hisham (d. 218 A.H). His edited version is the main source of most biographies. The English translation is by Alfred Guillaumme, The Life of Muhammad.

Was Ibn Ishaq trustworthy? He appears to be very careful in his writings. When in doubt, he frequently precedes a statement by the word "*Za'ama"* (he alleged). Another indication of his attempt at remaining objective is the use of the phrase, "*fi ma dhukira la"* (remembered or mentioned). Another phrase he uses often is "*fi ma balaghni*" (came to my knowledge). The account of Mi'raj is everywhere hedged with terms suggesting reservations and caution. After quoting both types of traditions that support "physical" or "spiritual" journeys, he makes the observation that it is immaterial whether the experience was real or visionary! Another phrase used is "Allah knows best."

Ibn Hisham, the Editor

A philologist of some repute, Ibn Hisham made useful and critical observations on the "poetry" cited in the *Sirah* and annotated it. However, he also appears to have abbreviated and sometimes even altered the original work. His over all contribution to Ibn Ishaq's original work is considered by most to be useful. Paradoxically Ibn Ishaq's biography of the Prophet ﷺ is commonly referred to as "*The Biography of the Prophet compiled by Ibn Hisham.*"

3. Ibn Jarar at-Tabari (d.923)

Another important source book frequently quoted is Abu Ja'far Muhammad ibn Jarar at-Tabari. This work called the Tarikh ar-Rusul wa al- Muluk (History of Prophets and Kings), is one of the monumental pieces of work compiled by the author.

Secondary Sources

1. Ali, Ameer. The Spirit of Islam: A History of the Evolution and Ideals of Islam with a Life of the Prophet. Amplified and revised, London: Chattos and Windus, 1964.
2. Armstrong, Karen. Muhammad: A Biography of the Prophet. Harper: San Francisco, 1992.
3. Andrae, Tor. Mohammed: the Man and His Faith. Translated from German by Theophil Menzel, New York, N.Y: Barnes and Noble, 1957.
4. Azam, Leila and Aisha Governor. The Life Of The Prophet Muhammad. London: Islamic Texts Society, 1985.
5. Azzam, Abdul Rahman. The Eternal Message of Muhammad. Translated from Arabic by Ceaser E. Farah; with an introduction by Vincent Sheean. New York: Devin-Adair Co., 1964.
6. Ghazi, Abidullah. The Life of Perfection. Skokie, IL: IQRA' International Educational Foundation, 1997.
7. Haykal, Muhammad Husayn. Life of Muhammad. Translated from Arabic by Isma'il Ragi al-Faruqi. Indianapolis, Indiana; American Trust Publications, 1976.
8. Irwing, Washington. The Life of Mahomet. London: J.M. Dent and sons, and New York: E.P. Dutton and Co., 1911.
9. Kelly, Marjorie. Islam. The Religious and Political Life of a World Community. New York: Praegers Publishers, 1984.
10. Lewis, Bernard. "Gibbon on Muhammad". In Daedalus, vol.105, no.3 (summer 1976): pp.89-101.
11. Lings, Martin. Muhammad; his life based on the earliest sources. Rochester, Vermont: Inner Traditions International, 1983
12. Nadwi, Syed Abul Hasan Ali. Muhammad; The Last Prophet: A Model for All Time. Leicester.U.K: Islamic Academy, 1993.

13. Nasr, Seyyed Hossein. <u>Muhammad Man Of God</u>. Chicago.IL: Kazi Publications, 1995.
14. Numani, Muhammad Shibli. *"<u>Allamah Shibli's Sirat an-Nabi</u>"*. Translated from Urdu by Fazlur Rahman. Karachi: Pakistan Historical Society, 1970.
15. Peters, F E. <u>Muhammad and the origins of Islam</u>. Albany, New York: State University of New York Press, 1994.
16. Raza, Ali Musa. <u>Muhammad in the Qur'an</u>. Lahore: Ashraf Printing Press, 1982.
17. Salahi, M.A. <u>Muhammad: Man and Prophet, A Complete Study of the Life of the Prophet of Islam</u>. Shaftesbury, Dorset: Rockport, Massachusetts, Brisbane, Queensland: Element, 1995.
18. Schimmel, Annmarie. <u>And Muhammad is His Messenger</u>. Chapel Hill, NC: University of North Carolina Press, 1985.
19. Von Denffer, Ahmad. <u>A Day with the Prophet</u>. Leicester, U.K: The Islamic Foundation, 1979.
20. Watt, William Montgomery. <u>Muhammad: Prophet and Statesman</u>. London: Oxford University Press, 1961
21. Zakariya, Rafiq. <u>Muhammad and the Qur'an. London:</u> Penguin Group, 1991.

Index

A

Abu Bakr 41, 55, 62, 63, 107, 114, 119, 120, 133, 138
Abu Hurayrah 67
Abu Jahl 55
Abu Talib 1, 33, 51, 52, 53, 54, 55, 138
Abyssinia 1, 50, 52, 55
Adhan 67
Ahl al-Kitab 41
Ahzab 2, 71
'Aishah 84, 119, 138, 141, 154
al-Lat, al-'Uzza, and al-Manat 32
Ali ibn Abu Talib 41, 47, 57, 62, 114, 138
Amr bin Awj 63
Ansar 61, 67, 73, 96, 97, 105
Arafat 157
Asbab an-Nuzul 107
'Awf 143
Aws 61, 65, 84, 143, 145, 146

B

Badr
    2, 18, 49, 71, 73, 74, 75, 76, 77, 78, 81, 105, 113, 135, 139
Banu Hashim 48
Bassiouni 76
Bayat ar-Ridwan 2, 94
belief system. 17
Bilal 49, 50
Buddha 10, 123, 124
Buddhism 31, 124
Bukhari 19, 97, 105, 121

C

Christianity 21, 23, 24, 31, 41, 51, 124, 140
Confucius 10
Conquest of Makkah 103
consultation 76, 79, 88, 125, 145
Covenant of Madinah 2, 3, 65, 96, 97, 134, 143

D

da'wah 47
Dawud (David) 134
Deification 25
Din 26, 118, 146

E

Economic Oppression 115

F

Farewell Pilgrimage 3, 118
fatrah 40
Fealty of Allah's Good Pleasure 94
Final Illness 119

G

Guillame 36, 58, 88, 99, 121

H

Hajj 61, 114, 115, 118, 157, 163
Hamzah bin Abdul Muttalib 50, 77
Hanif 33, 41, 55
Haykal 50, 58, 167
Hijab 57, 121
Hijrah 1, 2, 3, 18, 50, 62, 71, 84, 98, 114, 120, 133
Hira 34, 39
Hodgson 25, 48, 58

Hudaybiyah
　　2, 3, 91, 92, 94, 98, 103, 107, 113, 139, 147
Hunayn 3, 56, 86, 104, 105, 113, 114

I

Ibn Hisham 55
Ibn Ishaq 99, 159, 165, 166
Ibrahim (Abraham) 33, 41, 65, 71
Id al-Fitr 76
Ijma' 87
Injil 130
Isa (Jesus) 10, 31, 51, 95, 123, 124, 161, 165
Ishaq (Isaac) 36, 65, 99, 166
Ismail (Ishmael) 19, 58, 65, 167
Isra'/Miraj 1, 52, 53, 58, 166

J

Ja'far ibn Abi Talib 51
Jerusalem 22, 53, 71, 72
Jewish tribes 2, 18, 61, 65, 79, 80, 81, 83, 98, 144, 145
Jihad 3, 115, 116, 117, 126, 162
John E Woods 57
Judaism 41, 61

K

Ka'bah 33, 47, 71, 91, 96, 103, 113, 115, 159
Khadijah 34, 40, 41, 42, 48, 53, 131, 137, 141
Khalid ibn al-Walid 92
Khalifah (Caliph) 50, 57, 138
Khandaq 2, 18, 71, 78, 80, 83, 105, 113
Khaybar. 98, 131, 140
Khazraj 61, 65, 143
khul 109
Khuzah 98

L

Lat, al-Uzza, and al-Manat 32, 159

M

Madinah 18, 32, 54, 55, 61, 62, 63, 64, 65, 67, 68, 71, 72, 73, 76, 78, 79, 80, 81, 83, 91, 92, 94, 95, 98, 111, 132, 133, 143, 145, 146
Madinah. 18, 54, 73, 81, 111
Makkah 32, 33, 34, 47, 50, 51, 52, 54, 56, 61, 62, 63, 71, 83, 91, 92, 93, 96, 97, 98, 103, 104, 105, 111, 113, 126, 131, 139, 147, 162, 163
Makkah. 34, 48, 51, 62, 63, 162
Maria (the Copt) 95
marriages 3, 137, 138, 141, 142
Maryam (Mary) 51
Masjid an-Nabawi 64, 67
mawla 143
Migration 1, 2, 3, 50, 54, 55, 62, 63, 64, 68, 71, 73, 76, 79, 91, 95, 114, 118, 133
Mount Sur, 62
Muhajirun 67, 73, 96, 97
Mukhayriq 55
Munafiqun 80, 111, 135, 151
Musa (Moses) 73, 123, 165
Musab bin Umayr 62
Mus'ab bin 'Umayr 62
Mushrikun 131
Mut'im bin 'Adi 54

N

Nadir 81, 82, 83
Nafs 116
Negus 51, 52, 134, 140
non-Muslim friends 1, 54
Nuclear Family 84

O

Oaths of Aqabah 2, 61

P

Particularism 66
Peace Dividend 2
People of the Book 71, 80, 82, 83, 84
Pluralism 2, 64-66, 125
Pluralistic leader 2
Polygamy 32, 110
POWs 75, 76, 87, 125

Q

Qaynuqa 2, 81
Qiblah 2, 71, 72, 91
Qisas 88, 98, 113
Quraysh 18, 41, 47, 49, 51, 52, 55, 62, 71, 72, 73, 74, 76, 77, 78, 79, 82, 83, 91, 92, 94, 98, 103, 104, 113, 125, 132, 135, 137, 143, 144, 146, 147, 159
Qurayzah 2, 79, 82, 83

R

Rabi al-Awwal 120
Ramadan 34, 76, 134, 157, 162
Riba 32, 115, 116, 118

S

Sadaqah 116, 154
Salah 157, 161
Salman al-Farisi 79
Satanic Verses 3, 159
Sawm 76, 162
Shari'ah 163

Shura 76, 79, 87
statesman 2, 11, 18, 91, 95, 96, 97, 168
Status Of Women 108, 121
Stoic Optimist 1, 47
as-suffah 67

T

Tabari 72, 73, 99, 159, 166
Tabuk 110, 111
Tahannuf 34
Ta'if 32, 53, 54, 97, 105
Taqwa 117, 118, 121, 126
Tawhid 126, 159, 161
Tawrah (Torah) 83, 130
The Deep Thinker 1, 31
Tirmadhi 130, 131, 136
Treaty of Hudaybiyah 76, 91, 94, 103,
   107, 113, 134, 139, 147

U

Uhud 18, 55, 71, 76, 77, 78, 81, 86, 105, 113, 114, 139
'Umar ibn al-Khattab 50, 107, 120, 132, 138
Umm Salamah 107, 139
Ummah 2, 65, 66, 67, 143
Umrah 91, 98
Uthman ibn 'Affan 50, 93, 94, 138

W

Wahy 39, 40, 43, 63, 126, 134
Waraqah bin Nawfal 33, 55
Warrior 2, 71
wives 3, 67, 85, 106, 107, 138, 139, 141, 154
women in early Islam 3

Y

Ya'qub (Jacob) 65

Z

Zakah 116, 157, 163
Zayd 139
Zaynab 84, 85, 139, 140, 141
Zihar 32, 85, 109, 140
Zoroastrianism 31

About the Author

Dr. Javeed Akhter is a practicing physician and also a teacher and clinical researcher. Currently he is the director of Pediatric Pulmonology at the Hope/Christ children's hospital in Oak Lawn IL. He recently made the Chicago Magazine's year 2,000 edition of the "Top Doctors in Chicago".

He is a Clinical Associate Professor of pediatrics at the University of Illinois. In addition to the resident physicians in the program, he teaches medical students from University of Illinois, Chicago Medical School and Midwestern University. His medical research is primarily on asthma. Current research projects include "Inpatient Management of Asthma Using the Value Compass Tool," "Efficacy and Safety of Continuous Infusion of Magnesium Sulfate in Pediatric Status," and "Sensitivity and Specificity of Hemosiderin laden Macrophages in Broncho-Alveolar Lavage Fluid." He has several medical publications.

Self taught in Islamic studies, Akhter is widely read with a sound knowledge of Islamic fundamentals. The major influences on his thinking include the works of authors like Syed Abdul Latif (*The Mind Al-Qur'an Builds*), Maulana Azad (*Tarjumanul Qur'an*), Shibli Nomani (*Seera of Muhammad*), and Fazlur Rahman (*Major Themes of the Qur'an*).

He has been invited to give lectures and colloquia that include: "Muslims in America: an Analysis" at a ISNA conference in Chicago; "Islamic Medical Ethics" at the 1998 IMA convention in Seattle; and also at the MSAs of Northwestern University and Midwestern University, Chicago. He has spoken twice on "The Stereotyping of Muslims and Muhammad" at the Benedictine University, Lisle IL. He discussed the "Role of Muslim Think-Tanks in the US" at the 1998 ISNA convention in Chicago. He addressed the Northeastern University summer course on Islamic studies on "The Seven Phases of Prophet Muhammad's Life".

His publications include "An Etiological Analysis of the Heterodoxy among Muslims" *American Muslim* (reprinted in the KAC news letter); "The Exegesis of the Qur'an", *The Voice of Islam*; "The Quintessentials of the Islamic Belief System"

"The Nature and Structure of the Islamic World"; "A Pro-Active Vision for the Muslims in the US"; and "Muslims in America Opportunities and Challenges".

He is also the executive director of a Chicago-based Muslim think tank, the *International Strategy and Policy Institute*.